Living Architecture

English Translation: A. N. Wells

Living Architecture:
GOTHIC

TEXT: **HANS H. HOFSTÄTTER**

PHOTOGRAPHS: **RENÉ BERSIER**

Foreword: GUY DESBARATS

Macdonald · London

Editor of Series	Henri Stierlin
Plans	Jean Duret FAS SIA

SBN	356 031020
	Printed in Switzerland
Photo-composition	Filmsatz AG, Berne
Printing Text and Plans	Buri Druck, Berne
Heliogravure plates	Heliographia S.A., Lausanne
Offset reproductions	Aberegg-Steiner & Cie S.A., Berne
Binding	Max Grollimund, Basle

© Office du Livre
Fribourg 1970

Published in Great Britain in 1970 by
Macdonald & Co. (Publishers) Ltd.,
St Giles House, 49/50 Poland Street, London W.1.

Contents

Gothic Structures – a fruitful example

Foreword by Guy Desbarats, Architect

In the sixties of our century, now reaching their end, the imaginary museum of architecture holds a rich assortment of treasures. Images crowd closely upon one another, from the astonishing improvisations of the 'architecture without architect' of a Bernard Rudovsky to the deliberately seminal creations of a pavilion by Bronfman, by Mies van der Rohe or Phyllis Lambert. It would be vain to seek to determine here the clue of Ariadne which could show us a continuity of tendency or a really clear influence. Nevertheless, there are surprising and – for the committed architect – fruitful parallels to be drawn – parallels which, by analogy, throw light upon decisions which are as yet unclear.

Thus the recollection of a visit to Salisbury has remained live in my memory – a recollection which occupied my mind to an increasing degree. This Gothic example made me aware of the inadequacy of the contemporary synthesis between the endeavour to achieve a distinction of interior and exterior space on the one hand and the standardisation of industrial elements on the other – a synthesis which plays an ever increasing part in the determination of architectonic forms. It is my view that the architecture of today will achieve a fresh and dramatic unfolding when a new humanism, with a full consciousness of visual and perceptual pleasures, shall meet the demands of industrialisation. The tension born of this convergence stems from the difficult effort to do justice to new standards of hygiene and amenity while bringing them into harmony with the systematised results of technical and industrial innovations. In America, this state of affairs is described as 'socio-technical interface'.

The interest of the architect of today for the social sciences has led to an attempt to overcome the now all-too-complacent tendency towards universal space and the use of the 'curtain' wall. In place of the once so seductive temptation to plan simplified and universal spaces, we now have the complex analyses of programmes designed to produce strongly differentiated space-formations. With growing boldness, the architect strives to use a highly developed, soundly based technology in the service of the individual, in order to create an ambiance of beauty solely his own.

This development is clearly indicated by the electronic age by way of a quite unforeseen and – in view of the specialities and the multiplicity of the required production – remarkable flexibility of an industry which, thanks to automation, now no longer rules

George Frédéric's pavilion at Drummondtown, Quebec, by the architects Desbarats and associated

Theme-pavilions of the Expo 1967 at Montreal, partial view of the structures by the architects Desbarats and associated

man but is ruled by him. Shall we soon be able to shake off that 'will to power' which has found expression in architecture from the Italian renaissance down to the creations of American power-consciousness, and upon which a controlling will exerted its effect over a wide front? Shall we at last be able to return to a harmony of individual expression within the framework of a great collective creation, such as was possible in the time of Gothic art.

The technical achievements brought about by electronics in the service of advanced industrialisation encourage us to introduce into our all-too-starkly simplifying assimilations a broad spectrum of expressive variations. In the future, we shall even dare to attempt a synthesis of the higher demands which must be met in the construction of really new cities.

In Expo 1967, I attempted with my experiment in 'thematic' pavilions, to point a way in which such cities might achieve a consistent structure. In this sense, my project was based also upon the concept of an ideal Gothic, through which I wished to explore the capacity to create a variable structure, capable of extension, which should correspond to a flexible programme and through which spaces might be created which were always 'legible' and sometimes beautiful. The ever-growing part which this improvisation, this adaptation to new functions plays in the creative work of the architect, was known also – though marked by a far more leisurely rhythm – to the men of the Gothic age; as may be recognised from the fre-

quent changes of programme in the course of the building operations.

This ideal of a programme based upon the needs of men and realised in a changeable, expandable structure leads inevitably to the creation of more complex spaces, of differing heights, in sequences which become clear only through changes in the viewpoint of the observer – the product of considerations of volume, of light and of the inner 'atmosphere' for which the determining factor is not the plan of a façade but solely the worth of the building as a place to be inhabited.

This programme, so carefully adjusted to the varied needs of men, clearly corresponds to the possibilities of modern electronics. Now, too, there are certain materials at the disposal of the architect which,

Church of St. Thomas Aquinas at St. Lambert, Quebec, by the architects Desbarats and associated

through their plasticity and adaptability, go a long way towards meeting his new requirements.

The most important of these malleable materials are concrete and synthetic plastics. The use of pre-formed concrete – which in the last twenty years has become customary to an astonishing degree, opens up possibilities of controlled variations which the first great architects who used this material would hardly have dared to imagine.

The art, too, of facing with plastic materials and the treatment of surfaces by sand-blasting or glass-grinding, the use of pre-stressed concrete – all these offer far greater opportunities for expression than the simple juxtaposition of glass and steel surfaces.

Rhythmic forms and surfaces either rough or satin-smooth, according to choice, considerably widen the possibilities of architectural form. The very practical prefabrication process no longer leads solely to the construction of plain, starkly rectangular compositions. If the advance of science allows us to hope for a new synthesis between the viewpoint of human needs and that of materials, we may measure the success of our efforts against the Gothic dream.

Under the surface, Gothic still lives on and enriches to an astonishing degree every architecture, whenever a new generation rediscovers its heritage: it leads on, beyond all eclecticism, to a new merging, not of forms, but of the conceptions of growth, structure and light.

1. The Gothic Era

Periods of Gothic Art

In politics, sociology, and cultural history, the era contemporary with Gothic art is highly differentiated, heterogeneous and contradictory. Its span–more than three centuries–makes it doubtful whether one may speak at all of an era of the Gothic, let alone describe it as uniform. Rather, in the history of Gothic art, the following phases may be clearly distinguished:

An era of transitional style–that is to say, the supersession of the Romanesque, which begins in France around the middle of the twelfth century but first appears in Germany in and after the year 1200. The original impulse of this art emanates from the Ile-de-France and meets in neighbouring lands an artistic attitude certainly open to fresh tendencies, yet firmly founded upon the native architectural tradition: rather than submitting to the new ideas, it seeks to reconcile them with traditional conceptions. This is as true for the cultural regions of France as for the remaining European states; and hence it follows not only that every region finally develops its own form of the Gothic, but that architectural principles and details from the previous era survive in an almost anachronistic way.

The following period is distinguished by the building of great cathedrals: it could be described as the real age of the High Gothic, belonging essentially to the thirteenth century, though with variations in time throughout the individual countries. Characteristic of this period is the domination of architecture, which necessarily imposes itself upon all the other arts, and so reflects the entire cultural world.

This epoch is brought to an end in the fourteenth century by trends whose origin is mysterious; wars and epidemics spread over all Europe, causing great social misery and permitting only the fulfilment of a few great projects. The cathedrals at this time still unfinished remain mostly incomplete, or their completion stretches over centuries into the future; in many cases, the buildings have to wait the nineteenth century to attain the form which the builders of the

Middle Ages had foreseen for them. New ecclesiastical buildings, on the other hand, prefer the small undivided space-form which can be seen as a whole: the ever increasing role of the sermon makes it desirable to keep the congregation together, rather than disperse it in separate areas of the building. Religious life concentrates ever more intensely upon private devotions – upon the immediate encounter in prayer of man with God, and upon the heightened contemplation of the single image of a saint which can inspire such prayers. As a consequence, church architecture now releases the other arts more and more from its domination: statues are no longer confined to one place – and in particular not to the area of the doorway – but are in preference assigned to small chapels where only a few worshippers, who will not distract each other, may immerse themselves in their contemplation.

Here the image of the Gothic changes entirely, in a new and terminal phase. The release of painting and sculpture from the strict embrace of architecture leads to a basic change of stress. In the second half of the fourteenth century, the arts enter upon a new period of their development, of great importance for the future; from now on, they become the bearers of the new world-culture. Meanwhile, architecture itself scarcely changes – merely varying the already created space-concepts – though it often rises to splendid achievements and develops rich decoration. A basic alteration in church architecture only begins with the early Baroque, while the decorative forms of late Gothic still subsist in many places – especially north of the Alps – even into the early sixteenth century.

We have now outlined the problems that we shall tackle. The rise, change and development of new styles is, however, a question which can only be dealt with tentatively, since there are here too many different forces at work for a clear assessment. These forces may indeed be pointed out, but their function in the development of artistic expression can be counted among the enigmas of art. The accepted sign of Gothic architecture, the pointed arch, when considered purely from the architectonic point of view, doubtless represents an advance whose extent can be judged by the fact that it superseded the traditional round arch which had prevailed since Roman times.

This change, however, could almost be interpreted as a political one, since the succession of artistic styles was closely bound up with that of the imperial tradition. The new style was utilised by a power that in the first place competed with these imperial claims and was indeed later to supersede them.

High-points and Changes of Contemporary History

From the thirteenth century on, the political powers in Europe are in a state of change. With the last emperors of the ruling house of Hohenstaufen, the German Empire in Europe loses its dominating position and with it both the political and the spiritual leadership. After the death of Frederick II in 1250, Germany is split into territorial principalities. The interregnum lasts until the accession to the German imperial throne of Rudolph of Hapsburg, in 1273; but it was only under his second successor, Charles IV of Luxemburg, who ruled in Prague from 1347 to 1378, that the state of affairs in Germany became relatively so well ordered that a cultural flowering, too, became possible, even though limited in its effects to a small area of Europe.

As well as in Germany itself, the decline of the empire of the Hohenstaufens had its most important effects in Italy. In the middle of the tenth century, the first of the succession of emperors under the name of Otto had brought northern Italy under German rule; and from the beginning of the eleventh century, the conquest of southern Italy by the Normans was steadily advancing. The highpoint of the Norman rule in southern Italy was from 1130 to 1154, under Roger II. In 1162, Barbarossa overthrew and destroyed the rebellious Milan but suffered a decisive defeat at Legnano in 1176. Henry VI, who was an outstanding statesman and brought the Hohenstaufen empire to its highest point, succeeded, in 1194, in uniting the superbly organised Norman dominions with the Hohenstaufen realm. After his premature death – he died of malaria at the age of thirty-two – the structure of his empire abruptly broke up; and the development of a European system of nation-states began. Frederick II, the last Hohenstaufen emperor of importance, who was also King of Sicily, now resided only in his kingdom. His court was the centre of that Hohenstaufen renaissance which gave to the Italian Gothic its characteristic antique stamp, in which many have thought to see an anticipation of the renaissance of around 1500. It was, however, purely historical in nature, and finds its expression just as clearly in the architectural forms of the Apulian hunting seat, Castel del Monte, as in the pulpit reliefs of Niccolo Pisano, in Siena, which in their turn reach back to the many-figured, spatially animated relief style of the early antique sarcophagi. Through Frederick II, Sicily became the last foothold of the German imperial power and a typical example of the modern state. After his death, the Hohenstaufens were defeated in the struggle with Charles of Anjou, whose power embraced, from 1266 to 1284, the whole of southern Italy, including the capital, Naples, yet left behind it no impressive cultural traces.

In diametrical contrast to Germany, the rise of the French royal power at this time remained unbroken. In 987, the dominion of the Carolingians was succeeded by that of the Capets, which was to last until 1328. Its course is the exact reverse of that of Germany or Italy: out of a multitude of small states, ruled by powerful feudal masters who sometimes even wage war against the throne, there gradually grows up a united kingdom. Through clever political manœuvres, ever larger regions are incorporated in the royal domains, and even where the king is not the absolute ruler, his law, his organisation and his cultural influence prevail. The outward movement of the Gothic from the Ile-de-France into the provinces is an almost exact reflection of the gradual widening of the king's lands and influence. Its representation of the power and prestige of kingship bind the ruler closely together with the new architecture of the churches, which seem to express a higher approval of his claims to power. In cyclical representations, either three-dimensional, in the royal galleries of the façade, or in the stained glass of the windows, are

set out the ancestral succession and the history of the French kings, who now rival the claims to dominion of the early Hohenstaufens. Like that of the Hohenstaufens, the power of the Capets reaches finally back to Charlemagne and, through him, links them even with the emperors of Rome. The significance of the cathedral becomes even more closely bound up with the royal house through a strictly appointed sequence of ceremonies which the king completes, in so far as the cathedral becomes first the site of the coronation and the place of anointment (Rheims) and then the burial place (St. Denis) of the kings. Suger, abbot of St. Denis from 1122 to 1151 and for a time the national Chancellor, was a friend of the royal house: he outlined a comprehensive constructional concept which interpreted the meaning of the cathedrals.

The supplanting of German imperial might by French kingship was an important historical event. After the early death of the brilliant Hohenstaufen ruler, Henry VI, Germany was faced with a fateful double election, that split the country into two hostile camps, which were to be mutually weakened by centuries of civil war. This double election, however, was the result of a new political attitude: the traditional right of election after the succession, which was in reality merely a princely confirmation and not a genuine election, was now ousted by free elections by the princes. This independence within the kingdom nevertheless made Germany dependent upon neighbouring states; and this, for all practical purposes, brought the authoritarian autonomy of the empire to an end. One party, mainly in the northwest, chose in 1198 the Guelph, Otto IV of Brunswick – just sixteen years old and the son of Henry the Lion – as emperor. He was invested with the earldom of Poitou and, above all, financially supported in his wars by his uncle, Richard I of England. The other princely party simultaneously elected as emperor the youngest son of Barbarossa, Philip of Swabia, who stood in alliance with France. In the consequent struggle for the throne between Hohenstaufens and Guelphs, much valuable state property was dissipated among these respective allies. The recognition of Otto by Pope Innocent at first decided the contest in favour of the Guelphs. Otto's claim, however, collapsed through the secession of his supporters, so that the Pope was subsequently compelled to acknowledge Philip. When the latter was murdered, on account of a private affair, in 1208, there followed a fresh election of the Guelph, Otto IV. The struggle was complicated by manifold political entanglements – at first Otto, on account of his concessions to the Pope, was recognised by the latter and crowned; but later, because of his policy in southern Italy, he was excommunicated. The war was finally brought to an end in 1214 by the intervention of the French. The Battle of Bouvines, near Lille, between the French king, Philip Augustus, and Otto IV and his allies, ended in a French victory, with a double result: the end of the realm of Anjou and with it the recovery of the areas which had fallen to England through the marriage of Eleanor of Aquitaine to Henry II; and to some extent as a secondary result, the end of the struggle for the German imperial throne. In a splendid gesture, Philip Augustus sent to the young Hohenstaufen, Frederick II, who had played absolutely no part in the French victory, the imperial eagle which had been taken as booty, and thus simultaneously acknowledged the Hohenstaufen empire restored by him.

If Philip Augustus (Philip II) had begun the political rise of France, the mediaeval French kingdom was strengthened still further by Louis IX (Saint Louis) and later by Philip IV (Philip the Fair). Louis conquered the Provence and the earldom of Toulouse; Philip brought the papacy under his command, thereby greatly reducing those constraints under which the German Empire had chafed almost for centuries.

The history of England during the early and high mediaeval period was closely bound up with that of France, especially since England had continental territorial possessions on land that was part of France. The Battle of Bouvines, already mentioned, in which one of the two rival German emperors, Otto IV, in alliance with the English king, John 'Lackland', opposed the French, and in which the two allies were defeated, had decisive consequences also for England. In face of John's immoderate demands for money and his legal encroachments in his own country, the English barons under the leadership of Stephen Langton forced upon him, in 1215, the Magna Carta, a charter which laid down in sixty-four articles their rights as persons and as a class. The king, however, raised objections to this pre-democratic procedure and had Pope Innocent III declare the Charter invalid. It came to open war in England, in the course of which the barons offered the throne to the French Dauphin. Louis was in fact crowned in London in the year 1216. The civil war was ended by the death of John, in the same year, and by the Treaty of Lambeth, which recognised Henry III as the rightful king of England; but peace with France was concluded only in 1259, in Paris.

The political structure of Europe had been basically changed. The fourteenth century certainly saw a strengthened France but no united Europe. The concept of centralisation of the preceding centuries – which even yet was reflected in the great cathedrals, with their synthesis of worldly and spiritual power and breadth of dominion – was now broken. Cultural achievements no longer arise in broad programmes but are composed out of partial contributions from small individual centres which yet maintain mutual relations, exchange their thoughts and their successes and so, by means of cross-fertilisation, lead on to the broad development of a late mediaeval culture – one of the richest manifestations of western civilisation. It is quite wrong to regard this era as one of decline and cultural decadence – an autumnal period; it should far rather be looked upon as a splendid expansion of world culture, which achieved a far more marked degree of justice towards Nature and towards the individuality of Man than had any previous age.

The conflict between France and England flared up again with the death of Charles IV (Charles the Fair), in 1328, as the main line of the Capets was extinguished. King Edward III of England (1327–77) believed that as the son of a daughter of Philip the Fair he had more claim to the French throne than Philip VI, of the House of Valois, son of Philip's brother.

In 1338 there broke out the Hundred Year's War between the two countries. At first, England achieved important successes, but both countries were fighting not merely against their external enemies but also with internal troubles and revolts. By the short-lived Treaty of Bretigny (1360), France was compelled to yield the entire south-west and in the north, Calais and the earldom of Ponthieu. Charles V, The Wise, recovered from the English all these regions with the exception of Calais, Bordeaux, and Bayonne. By his marriage to the daughter of Charles VI, Henry V of England obtained from the French by the Treaty of Troyes (1420) following his victory at Agincourt, recognition as the heir and regent of France, and matters again took a turn strongly favourable to the English. But Henry died early and under his son, Henry VI, these successes ebbed away. Joan of Arc, The Maid of Orleans, had roused French national feeling afresh and around the middle of the fifteenth century the war between the two countries came to an end without the conclusion of any official treaty. The English were able to maintain their rule solely in Calais and in the Channel Islands.

In the second half of the fifteenth century, England was again politically weakened by the Wars of the Roses, between the houses of York and Lancaster, and France was able to widen her victory. Louis XI (1461–83) subdued Burgundy, which was also claimed as their inheritance by the Hapsburgs, and over which war between France and the Hapsburgs smouldered on for decades. Anjou and Provence fell to the crown territories and at the end of the fifteenth century only Brittany and Flanders remained outside the kingdom.

Also in the areas of German rule, whose fate was now less dependent upon those of France and England, power was divided among various groups. Rudolph of Hapsburg (1273–91) had been able to restore the imperial power to some extent. With Charles IV, whose seat of government was in Prague and who was crowned emperor by the Pope, the electoral principle was broken and the imperial throne was inherited within the house of Hapsburg: formally, the rights of the electors remained in being but in practice the system proved unworkable. Through astute dynastic politics – and more especially by the peaceful road of marriage and inheritance – the Hapsburgs built up in the late mediaeval period an imperial realm which extended as far as Spain and on which, as was said by Charles V, the sun never set.

The Papacy in the Middle Ages

The ecclesiastical state exerted a decisive influence upon both the political and the spiritual development of the West, since it laid claim to the primacy of the spiritual over the temporal power. Under Innocent III (1198–1216) the power of the papacy reached its zenith. He directly strengthened the political independence of the ecclesiastical state and claimed sovereignty over Sicily – which he was even able to exercise for a time. Then he intervened in the political affairs of almost every country, with the aim of establishing a unified western Christendom, to meet the threat of Islam and the Mongols upon Europe's frontiers. Never had a pope possessed so much political influence as Innocent. By over-emphasis of his claims to political power, however, he laid the foundations of wide and varied opposition to the papacy which had its full effect only after the end of his period of rule. The Lateran Synod of 1215 was the triumph of his papacy, when spiritual and temporal leaders of the entire Christian West were gathered together under his chairmanship. The idea of the unity thus demonstrated becomes visible in the great cathedral buildings of the thirteenth century, in which not only religious but also secular ceremonial found its place under the aegis of the church.

The most important points of the synod of 1215 were as follows: a demand for the reform of the church, whose necessity was at this time freshly underlined by the foundation of the new orders of Franciscans and Dominicans; establishment of the teaching on transubstantiation according to which the substances of the bread and wine in the mass were completely transformed into those of the body and blood of Christ; the demand that confession and communion should be performed at least once a year; restriction upon the foundation of further orders; the enforcement of the apostolic rules for the avoidance of the formation of heretical sects, which were to be pursued and rooted out by the most radical methods;

restrictions upon episcopal indulgences and a ban upon the imposition of taxes on church property without the consent of the pope, in order to ensure the independence of the monasteries and of the bishops from the temporal power. The doctrine of transubstantiation led to a new element in the service, the 'elevatio', or raising up and showing of the transformed substances to the people. The wish expressed here to make visible and to show is a strong causative element in the entire development of imagery in the cathedrals.

If the apogee of papal power was reached in the thirteenth century, then the nadir is to be found in the fourteenth; and from it the church was unable to recover appreciably even in the fifteenth century. Disputes similar to those between the Vatican and the German emperors followed in the fourteenth century between the Vatican and Philip the Fair. His chancellor, Nogaret, supported Philip's aims with regard to a national church; and in 1303 he tried to remove the pope by an attempted assassination at Anagni. The pope survived the attack, but died shortly afterwards in the same year.

Under pressure from the Capets, a native Frenchman, Bertrand de Got, hitherto Archbishop of Bordeaux, was chosen as pope; but, as it was feared that this 'French' pope would not be safe in the Vatican, he was brought to Avignon. Through him and his successors, who had their seat in Avignon from 1309 to 1377, the papacy of the period fell into close political dependence upon France. Later, because the Italians resented the absence of the pope from home, a threat developed to the Papal States; and eventually Gregory XI returned to Rome in 1377 and henceforth ruled from the Vatican – not, as had earlier popes, from the Lateran.

The Dance of Death as the Fate of an Age

It is obvious that this period no longer had the staying power to build cathedrals. The church was lacking in self-confidence and the people in the material means necessary for great building projects. The wars weakened every class. In addition, there came the chastisements which were foretold by the reformers and penitential preachers as retribution for the corruption of the church and the sins of the people: from 1315 to 1317 a famine oppressed all Europe; from 1340 to 1350 the Black Death spread over the entire continent. It exacted many millions of victims, – whole generations, villages and regions – almost a third of the entire population of the West. The plague took its deadliest toll in the harbours of the Mediterranean; but it extended also to inland cities on the great trade routes, such as Saragossa, Toulouse, Paris, Basle, Cologne, Frankfurt and Magdeburg – terrible peaks in its dread career. In the cities, lay sisterhoods and brotherhoods were formed for the burial of the dead. Scarcely had it died away than the pest flared up again in 1380–81; and even in the periods of its temporary absence, it stood like a spectre of dread before the minds of the people. The performances of the Dance of Death which survived into the sixteenth century gave expression to their fear.

Brotherhoods of flagellants called for public repentance. These were associations of people seized with religious fervour, who marched through the land and through the cities, with bared backs, beating one another with whips. As they went, they sang psalms and penitential hymns which played a part in the development of early religious folk songs. Since they denounced the neglect of duty of the clergy, their movement was forbidden first by Pope Clement VI and later by the Council of Constance in 1417. In the whole movement, whether lawful or unlawful, the new participation of laymen in the world of religious ideas finds strong expression.

Social Changes

In the social structure of the Middle Ages, three basic groupings are quite clearly distinguishable, corresponding to the historical division into an early, a high, and a late mediaeval period. The dominant factor in the early Middle Ages was an aristocracy built upon the tradition of the old German nobility of lineage and the Roman and Romanic senatorial families. This aristocracy held both the political and the ecclesiastical offices; it guarded jealously and heroically the spirit of tradition and was strongly

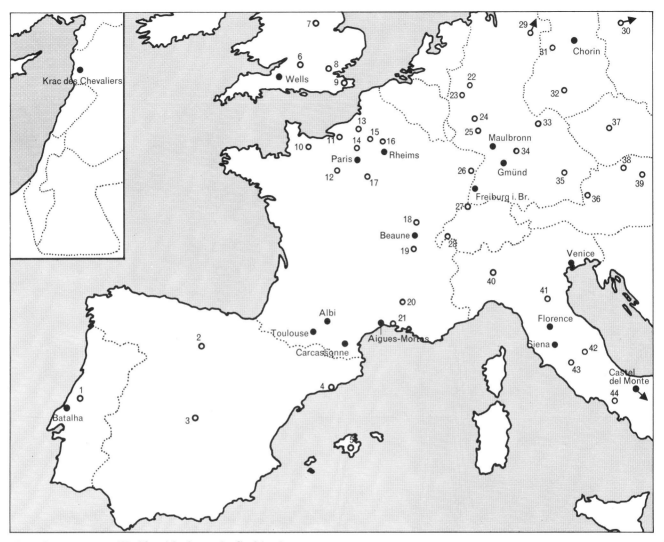

Map of the Western World, with the main Gothic sites
mentioned in the text:

1 Tomar	10 Caen	19 Cluny	28 Lausanne	37 Prague
2 Burgos	11 Jumièges	20 Avignon	29 Lübeck	38 Zwettl
3 Toledo	12 Chartres	21 Stes-Maries-de-la-Mer	30 Danzig	39 Vienna
4 Barcelona	13 Amiens	22 Soest in Westphalia	31 Magdeburg	40 Milan
5 Majorca	14 Saint-Denis	23 Cologne	32 Naumburg	41 Bologna
6 Oxford	15 Noyon	24 Mainz	33 Bamberg	42 Assisi
7 Lincoln	16 Laon	25 Worms	34 Dinkelsbühl	43 Orvieto
8 London	17 Sens	26 Strasburg	35 Landshut	44 Fossanova
9 Canterbury	18 Citeaux	27 Basle	36 Salzburg	

conservative. In the development towards the high mediaeval period, the base of this pyramid of nobility, at whose apex stood the king, became ever more widely extended. The maintenance of an administrative apparatus of skilled officials and of a trained army was made possible only by rewarding those entrusted with these tasks, with land, privileges and guarantees of immunity which gradually established themselves as hereditary. At the same time, with the transfer of property from the crown to the aristocracy, the power of the ruler was restricted and reduced. The economic – and thus in many cases also the political – power of the king was dependent upon the revenue from his private estates. The aristocratic feudal lords exercised, upon their own territories, the powers of state in every sense of the words. True, they were bound by liege-loyalty to the king – above all, in any military activities – yet for their part, they could play a most effective role in determining the policy of the crown. Especially towards the end of the feudal period proper, which extends in Europe from the ninth to the end of the fourteenth centuries, the conflicts resulting in all these countries from this feudal situation are apparent in the history of the period. We have already spoken of them in preceding paragraphs.

In the late Middle Ages – parallel to the period of the Gothic – certain forces make their appearance, but their origins could certainly be observed considerably earlier. In the twelfth and thirteenth centuries, the middle class was beginning the struggle for its economic existence and for its freedom; while in the fourteenth and fifteenth centuries, it already determined the level of material and cultural civilisation to an ever increasing degree. A considerable rise was achieved by broad categories of the population; and in the cities there began to form a new social stratum, conscious of its status and politically to be reckoned with. Its artistic expression is to be found in the late mediaeval city culture which often sets itself up, with a fuller freedom and independence, in the place of the old feudal culture. The changed situation is reflected in church architecture. The cathedrals of the high mediaeval rulers were closely bound up with the purposes of the state – as royal cathedral, burial

place, or site of official court ceremonies or gatherings of state – and were built by compulsory labour. Later on the citizens undertook the work in common, linking the house of God to their particular purposes, as a city landmark, as a place of jurisdiction, or for private devotions in the chapels furnished by propertied families. The buildings were now more modest in their proportions but not less beautiful. From the side of the church, there was considerable participation by the reformed monasteries – such as those of the Cistercians – and the orders of mendicant friars, whose spiritual care for the people corresponded to a new care for religion and who also, in accordance with this religious spirit, created new places of worship.

The Place of Piety in the General World View

To correspond with the social changes, there were also necessarily changes in the devotional attitude of the people and in the efficacy of the spiritual care by the church itself. In the early Middle Ages, the church was just as absolute as the state – above all in the self-confidence of her unassailable cultural plan, which so decisively prevented all attacks and all criticism that even the inheritance by tradition of anti-christian currents of thought – which must certainly have exerted an after-effect from pre-christian times – now ceased. The situation changed in the high mediaeval period, when public attacks could no longer be ignored and voices calling for the reform of the church became ever more insistent. In the Romanesque period, the church began to accept the reality of the devil, in that it accorded him a fixed place in its structure and thereby tamed and overpowered him: demons were 'chained' to the gates, served the virtuous saints as footstools or the font as a pedestal. There and nowhere else, as the conquered, finally harnessed in the service of the saints, they were able to maintain their existence. Thus they became the lowest elements in a mighty structure of doctrine which manifests itself to the full in the cathedrals of the thirteenth century.

Scholasticism and the Cathedral

In its dimensions, the cathedral is designed for the masses in an age which will not simply accept the Christian faith preached to it: on the grounds of the widening knowledge of the ancient authors and in the field of the natural sciences, the people of this age desire so to understand the faith that it shall include within itself the new scientific world-view. From the end of the twelfth century, Paris begins to develop as the central point of European culture. Here lived Abelard and Thomas Aquinas and from every part of the Christian world came streams of learned men and their pupils. Out of the relationship of Greek philosophy and Christian belief there arose the conception of a world-view whose basis was 'notional realism', that is, the doctrine that an object is never simply what it appears to be, but the symbol and sign of a higher reality.

Around 1200, teachers and pupils founded a community of scholars which was recognised by Philip Augustus and by Innocent III, and its statutes were sanctioned in 1213. Thus there was founded in Paris a university like the contemporary communities of scholars in Bologna, Oxford and Cambridge. In the following period, similar institutions arise all over Europe. All the scientific thought of the time goes to produce great syntheses, in which the knowledge of the age is encyclopaedically gathered together and united under a single, consolidating theological viewpoint. By 'scholasticism' should be understood mediaeval philosophy in the narrower sense – that which defines its purpose as follows: 'The scholastic method seeks to achieve, by the application of reason to the truths of revelation, the highest possible insight attainable by philosophy into the nature of belief, in order thus to bring home to the thinking mind of Man the substance of supernatural truth and to make possible a united, systematic and comprehensive representation of the truths of salvation, so that the objections raised against these truths may be refuted.' (Grabmann). This, then, is not a search for truth, since that is established from the beginning; the philosophic effort is merely to understand that truth. To know means to meditate upon the God-given reality in the form of propositions and inferences. The world is comprehended in formulae and definitions; the rich variety of the creation is classified and described and rendered present in the representational cycles of the cathedrals: so too, human activity, from manual through intellectual work to philosophy and theology, the overthrow of vice by the virtues and finally the history of mankind from its creation to its last day. In accordance with the spirit of piety of the thirteenth century, the meaning of the cathedral lies in the complete representation of everything included in the faith.

Mysticism and Private Devotions

As the thirteenth century runs out, contradictions to scholasticism are asserting themselves, emphasising the distinction between philosophy and theology and thus foreshadowing modern thought. The scientific and theological discussions in the University of Paris – still the centre of intellectual dissemination in Europe – culminate in the idea of uniting humanity under the one law of a single, all-comprehending truth. But as against this large-scale doctrinal structure of scholasticism and its testimony for God, scepticism begins to make itself felt even among the theologians. It is impossible to prove the existence of God and therefore one must experience it; this is the fundamental view of the mysticism which tries to show the way to unity of the human soul with God through an intense emotional experience.

The Dominican monk, Master Eckhart (1260–1327), a teacher in Paris and Provincial of the Dominicans in Saxony, provided in his works so serious a counterweight to scholasticism that he was suspected of heresy and persecuted; and after his death, passages were officially struck out of his writings. He preached detachment from everything earthly, as a pre-condition for the purification of Man, whose final goal is absolute tranquillity and peace in God. His preachings and hymns of consolation and meditation show an undreamt-of power of language, new words, phrases and concepts, startling images. The writings of the Dominican monk, Henry Suso belong to the most widespread mystical thought of the Middle Ages. In his meditations upon the suffering of Christ and dialogues between Man in search of God and the personification of wisdom, he makes use of the lyrical tones, full of pity, of the 'Minnesinger'. The book of meditations of Thomas a Kempis, 'De Imitatio Christi', also calls for an intuitive understanding, through meditation, of Christ's suffering and his way of redemption. With Birgitta of Sweden (1303–73) and Katherine of Siena (1347–80), this intuitive understanding leads to direct visions which have a deep influence upon the piety of the age.

This piety seeks for new places and new images for devotional purposes. Personal dialogue with God or meditation upon sacred subjects makes the presence of great crowds entirely inadmissible and demands a small, narrowly confined space whose atmosphere favours such intuitions. So now there appear, for preference, churches with such small spaces; and the already existing cathedrals have built on to them little intimate chapels that afford room for such private devotions. The great cyclical representations of the teaching of salvation, which are far too spacious to be comprehended by the individual eye, give place to the so-called 'devotional image', which takes a single incident from its historical context and sets it before the worshipper, upon the altar. It is at this time that we find the rise of the 'pieta', the group of Christ with St. John, the merciful Christ and the Man of Sorrows, which often veritably compel the emotion of pity in the worshipper. The ascetic side of mysticism is reflected not only in the plastic form of the figures, which now renounces its hardly won representational truth and renders them hollowed out and distorted by unrealistic curves, but also in the relationship to the mass of the building. The pillars, responds, and the groining of vaults are grooved and hollowed by chamferings, the windows are tall and narrow, and now, in place of three-dimensional masses, it is space and shadowed outlines that speak most clearly.

Middle Class Piety

Mysticism rules the entire fourteenth century – a period disastrously laid waste by war and plague and afflicted by material uncertainty. With the stabilisation of city culture in the fifteenth century, the attitude of piety changed once again. In accordance with the claim of the middle class to its own private sphere, the importance of private devotion is maintained; private fortunes now allow even more than before the personal possession of saintly images. At the same time, the new sense of reality with which the middle class grasps its world and the objects therein is carried over even into religious events, and these are represented with the aid of the newly won reality. As in the time of the cathedrals, there now sets in a new enthusiasm for images, which causes everything to be rendered visible and makes the facts of the faith understandable by transferring them into its own time – just as if these things could happen even 'today' – so that they may manifest both their actuality and, at the same time, their eternal significance. Church architecture likewise serves the new middle class municipality; in many cases it becomes again great and representative, planned as a city landmark and as a place in which the community may experience its solidarity. More frequently than before, the architectural type of the hall-church is preferred, since it gives expression spatially to the new feeling of flocking together and of wholeness. The former costly design of figures around the doors is renounced; in its place, the late Gothic carved altar, with side pieces, now gathers around it the representations of the salvation story and sets up a recognisable centre within the architectural whole. As in the time of the cathedrals, all levels of the population work together upon the building and make possible its fitting out and furnishing; but no longer as anonymous helpers – rather with a proud awareness of status to which the images and inscriptions of the founders bear witness.

Plates

Rheims: Cathedral (France)

21 View down the central axis, from the eastern choir chapel, of the hemi-cycle of columns which separate the choir of the cathedral from the ambulatory. Between the two central columns, the view extends down the nave to the west wall.

22 The area of the vaulting, above the high windows of the nave. Clearly visible is the way in which the ribs and the transverse arches which separate the bays grow out of the rising responds.

23 Detail of the triforium, between the ground-floor arcades and the clerestory windows. In the wall behind, a relieving arch can be seen which carries the weight of the wall above on to the pillars.

24 Diagonal views through the cathedral – seen here from the south transept, through the arcades to the nave – always produce a variable effect in which the parallel lines seem to fall of their own accord into a rhythmic order.

25 Upward view into the area of the triforium on to the southern and eastern walls of the choir. The function of the triforium – to bring about the apparent dissolution of the wall surface as a boundary to space – is here particularly clear.

26 The great west rose-window of the cathedral. A spandrel window occupies the space immediately below the keystone of the vaulting, thus enabling the window as a whole to take on an ogival shape.

27 A view through from the south aisle to the interior of the west wall, which is relieved throughout the whole width of the nave and side aisles by niches – divided horizontally by foliage in relief.

28 In the exterior, as in the interior, the mass of the wall surface is relieved as far as possible – here by closely set arcades, punctuated by projecting, triangular niches.

29 View of the flying buttresses, with the central supports which make possible the bridging of the wide gap before the outer abutments.

Albi: Cathedral of St. Cecily (France)

30 The cathedral from the north-west. In the foreground, the river Tarn; to the right of the picture, the old, fortified city wall; between it and the cathedral, the fortress-like mediaeval palace of the bishop.

31 View into the tower of the cathedral.

32 Detail of the eastern exterior wall, showing the juxtaposition of cubic and prismatic surfaces of brick-work.

33 The defensive passage which crowns the walls of the cathedral.

34 The interior of the cathedral is articulated by tall and deeply cut niches. The horizontal division by a gallery is an addition of the late Gothic period.

Paris: Sainte-Chapelle

35 View from the south-west of the chapel, in the courtyard of the present Palais de Justice, the former royal palace.

36 The upper chapel displays one of the boldest treatments of wall surface to be found anywhere. The area is reduced to a framework of vaulting shafts and the transparently luminous coloured surface of the windows. In the interior, one can forget the powerful, external buttresses that assure the solidity of this apparently fragile system of supports.

37 Vaulting in the eastern section of the hall-like upper chapel.

Toulouse: the Jacobin Church

38 View to the south-west through the south aisle of the twin-aisled hall-church.

39 The 'palm tree' column closes the row of central piers at the east end.

40 Detail of the impost block of the 'palm tree' pier, point of departure of the vault ribs.

Albi, Cathedral of St. Cecily
Plan 1:1000, interior elevation of one bay and transverse
section of the nave 1:500, axonometric construction

N

01 5 10   20   30   50
M
FT
0 10 20   50   100   150

0 1   5   10   20
M
FT
0 10 20   50

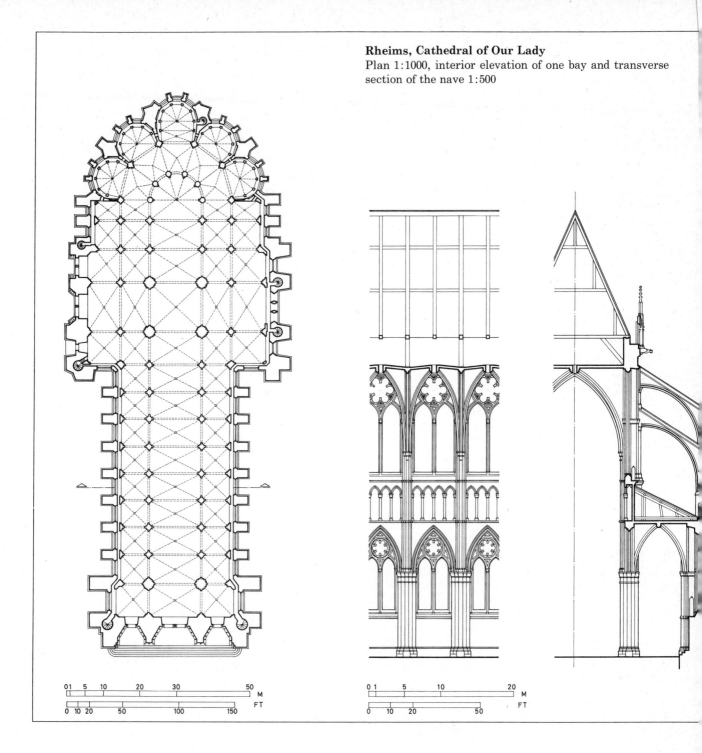

Rheims, Cathedral of Our Lady
Plan 1:1000, interior elevation of one bay and transverse
section of the nave 1:500

Notes

Survey of the principal Gothic Cathedrals of France

St. Denis, Abbey. Founded by Abbot Suger. Two tower façade, 1137–40, towers after 1144. Perpendicular threefold division by projecting buttresses, small rose-window. Choir with double ambulatory and radiating chapels 1140–43 (only the lower portion preserved). Upper part of choir and the nave 1231–81; glazed triforium.

Sens, Cathedral. Around 1140–64, later transept from the beginning of the 14th, 15th and 16th centuries. Linked system and sexpartite ribbed vaulting in the nave. Clerestory windows enlarged in the 13th and 14th centuries.

Noyon, Cathedral. Choir with ambulatory and radiating chapels begun around 1150; nave after 1170. The first internal elevation in four parts of a vaulted building, with a triforium in part blind. The originally sexpartite vaulting in the linked system was replaced after 1295 by quadripartite vaulting. Transept with semicircular terminations.

Senlis, Cathedral. 1153–91, transept mid-13th century. Threefold division of wall elevation, with linked system. Choir with ambulatory and radiating chapels.

Laon, Cathedral. 1170–1210, about 1190 modification of the system of supports and elongation of the choir, with flat east end. Sexpartite vaulting, elevation in four parts, transept with two aisles. West front erected between 1190 and beginning of 13th century. Large, central rose-window. Raising of the central portion. Powerful spatial formation of the tower through octagonal core and addition of diagonally set canopied projections on four sides. Influence on Bamberg.

Paris, Cathedral of Notre-Dame. Choir, with double ambulatory but without chapels, begun about 1163, completed about 1182; transept does not project. About 1190, nave in five aisles, with a four-part elevation, in which oculi replace the triforium. Alterations to the interior about the middle of the 14th century and after. Construction of chapels surrounding the entire cathedral; enlargement of the clerestory windows through merging with the oculi. Addition of the transept façades (Jean de Chelles). West-front after 1215, with dominating horizontal articulation and large rose-window.

Bourges, Cathedral. Choir 1172–1218, consecration 1324. Additions and completions 14th–16th centuries. Five aisles without transept; elevation in three parts with very high arcades and unusually low clerestory windows. Inner side aisles with own light (windows). Sexpartite vaulting without alternation of supports; angular piers with pilasters.

Chartres, Cathedral. Rebuilt in Gothic, 1194–1260. Cruciform ground-plan. Single nave with two side aisles; widely projecting choir and double ambulatory. Alternation of large and small choir chapels. Elevation in three parts. Alternation of composite piers. High-nave windows in two parts, with rose-window above. Buttressing for the first time as an independently impressive element.

Soissons, Cathedral. South transept with elevation in four parts, about 1180–1200. Choir 1200–12; nave with elevation in three parts. Directly influenced by Chartres.

Rheims, Cathedral. (See description in text pp. 81–7.)

Rouen, Cathedral. Nave after 1200. Three-part elevation with large, blind gallery openings. Richly moulded, clustered-column piers, with slender responds.

Dijon, Notre-Dame. About 1225–40. Burgundian Gothic. Choir without ambulatory or chapels. Three-part elevation, sexpartite vaulting. Buttressing reduced, wall reinforced.

Beauvais, Cathedral. Choir 1246–75. Widening, increase in the intervals between piers, narrowing of the side aisles, raising of all areas. After collapse of vaulting, introduction of intermediate piers and sexpartite vaulting. Nave after 1500.

Metz, Cathedral. From middle of the 13th century, nave 1327–81, transept and choir 1486–1520. Dense tracery of clerestory windows; bold exterior buttressing.

Coutances, Cathedral. Nave after 1218. Elevation in three parts of almost equal importance. Norman arrangement of coupled columns in choir. Massive west end construction, square crossing-tower and solid wall structure of the whole carry on Norman tradition.

Albi, Cathedral. (See description in text pp. 89–91.)

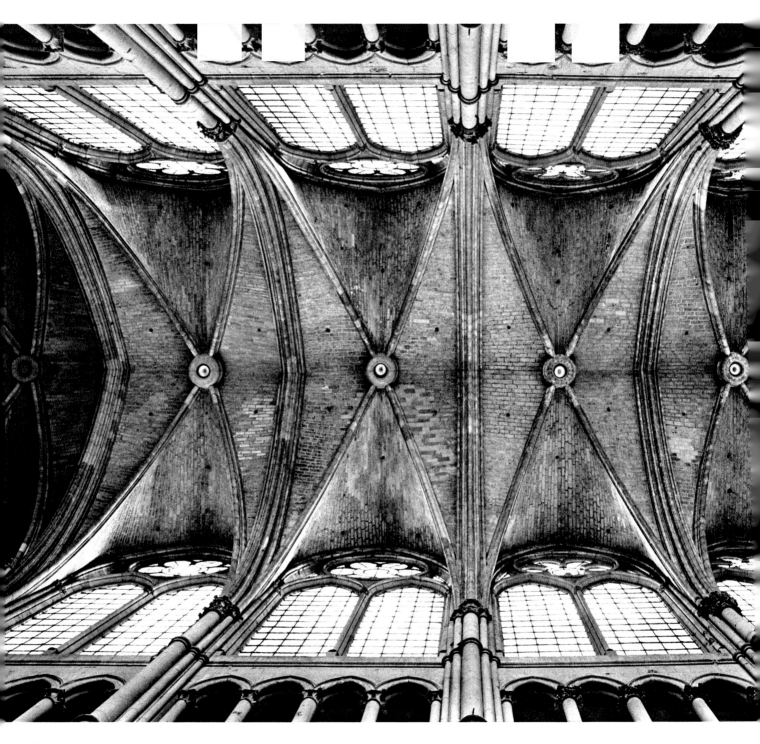

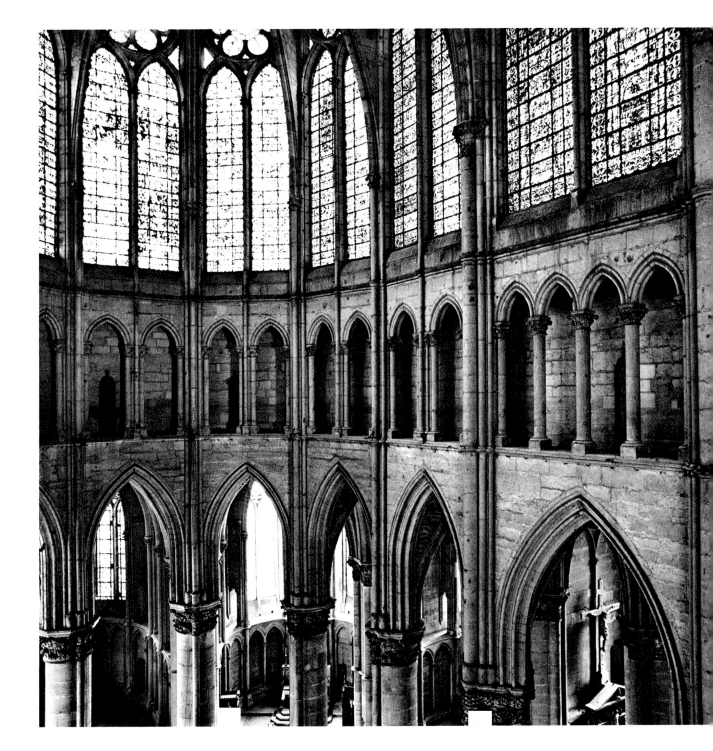

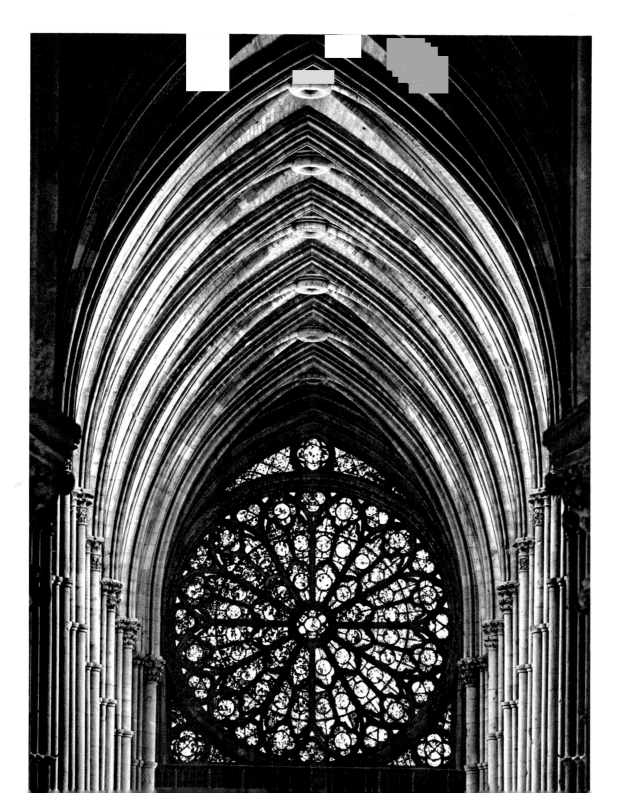

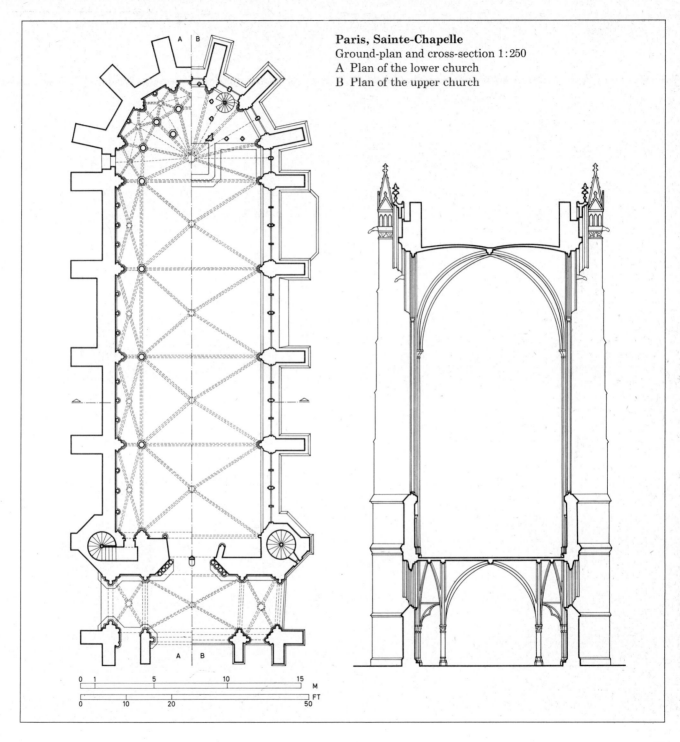

Paris, Sainte-Chapelle
Ground-plan and cross-section 1:250
A Plan of the lower church
B Plan of the upper church

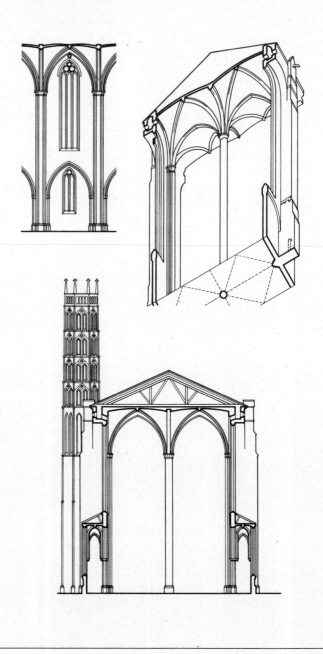

Toulouse, the Jacobin church
Ground-plan, cross-section, elevation of the nave and iso-metric view 1:600

2. The Cathedral as Model

Gothic – the Word and the Idea

The word 'Gothic' as a descriptive designation of the style of a period, was coined in an age which claimed to have achieved the overthrow of the Middle Ages. Closely bound up with the term, therefore, is the intention to express the imperfection of this bygone era in relation to that age itself. The Renaissance knew three great divisions in the cultural development of the West: the Antique, which set the criterion for all later art; the barbaric period of the Middle Ages, in which the antique standards were lost; and the New Age, which was striving to attain once more the ancient ideal. In essence, Giorgio Vasari (1511–74) gave its stamp to the conception of Gothic art which ruled until nearly the end of the eighteenth century; and for him, of all the 'barbarian tribes' from the time of the migrations, who broke in from beyond the Alps upon the antique culture, the Goths were familiar as having the most corrupting effect upon taste. 'This accursed design is followed even in those many little boxes with which the buildings are covered on all sides and in every area: one thing is piled on top of another, and in every case furnished with a multitude of ornamental obelisks, spikes and leaves. By themselves producing an unsettled effect, when combined in such involuted forms these boxes possess no sort of stability; they seem far rather to be constructed out of paper than from stone or marble. Everywhere there are projections, kinks, consoles and interlaced garlands, so that all proportion and harmony are lost.'

In the eighteenth century, Johann Georg Sulzer (1720–79), in his 'General Theory of the Fine Arts', not only took over Vasari's judgment but provided for it even more detailed grounds: 'If you take a man basely born and brought up among the mob and make him suddenly great and rich and he then tries to imitate distinguished people in his clothing, in his manners, in his houses and gardens and in his whole way of life – then in all these things he will be Gothic. The Gothic constitutes an ostentatious expenditure, totally without taste, upon works of art which are not lacking in substance – not always, even, in size and splendour – but always in the beautiful, the agreeable and the refined. Since this lack of taste can show

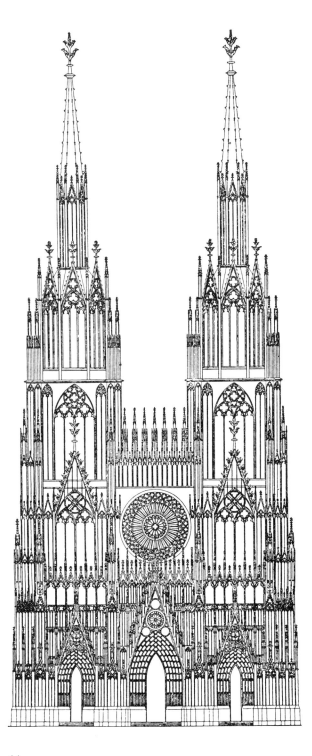

itself in many ways, so too, the Gothic can be of various kinds... Altogether, it seems therefore that the Gothic taste arises from lack of reflection upon the thing that is to be made.

Yet the change in estimation came about even in Sulzer's time. It is from Goethe that we have the first favourable judgment upon Gothic architecture, written in 1772, under the influence of his impressions of Strasburg cathedral: 'As I went for the first time to the cathedral, my head was full of the common understanding of good taste... Under the rubric, "Gothic", as though in the appropriate section of a dictionary, there heaped themselves up all the synonymous misunderstandings – "vague", "disorderly", "forced", "patched up", "botched", "overloaded" – that had ever run through my head, so that I shuddered as I went, at the prospect of some malformed, bristling monster. How unexpected, therefore, was the feeling with which my first glimpse of it astonished me! A mighty impression filled my soul, for though it was made up of a thousand details, all in harmony, so that I could very well taste and enjoy it, yet I could in no way recognise it or explain it... How often have I returned in order to view – from all sides, from every distance and in varying states of light its dignity and splendour.'

The Romantic period opened the way to an understanding of the Middle Ages; and even Gothic architecture thus attained, in the first two decades of the nineteenth century, a favourable standing in the history of artistic styles. It was recognised that a mediaeval Christian art must be built upon assumptions totally different from those of classical antiquity; but that it was nevertheless just as strictly related to the realities of belief and the effects of popular conceptions of the world and the hereafter. And so at last people began to understand Gothic art in its own right and not through the comparison with the monuments of ancient architecture. Around the middle of the century begins the scientific discussion of the Gothic. In the 'Vienna Journal of Architecture', in 1843, Fr. Mertens explains, with scientific

Strasburg, cathedral: façade

method, the development of the Gothic in France. In France itself, research concentrates above all upon the technical factors. The most important work is accomplished by the restorer of many mediaeval monuments in France, Emmanuel Viollet-le-Duc (1814–79), who presented his results in the second volume of his 'Dictionnaire Raisonné de l'Architecture Française du XIᵉ au XVIᵉ Siècle', which began to appear in 1854. Published in Germany at about the same time, 'The History of Architecture' by Franz Kugler (1808–58), deals in the third volume with the Gothic, and already presents a far-reaching survey of the Gothic buildings in every country of Europe. With the appearance of the basic work of Georg Dehio and Gustav Bezold, 'The Ecclesiastical Architecture of the West', the foundation is laid for the researches of the twentieth century. These have led – in France, primarily through Marcel Aubert, Emile Mâle and Henri Focillon, in Germany through Ernst Gall, Hans Jantzen, Kurt Bauch and Hans Sedlmayr – to great comprehensive accounts. On the basis of their researches, we now understand the Gothic as a mighty synthesis of the new attitude of the Christian faith and a unique architectural technique.

The Primary Form of the Cathedral

The primary form of the church – upon which the form of the cathedral is based – and the intrinsic meaning of the house of God were developed under the Christianity of the late antique period.

The basic type of cathedral architecture is the basilica, which developed in the time of Constantine from the Roman secular building of a market hall and hall of justice into a Christian church. It is a building of longitudinal space, with three or more parallel structures, separated from one another by columns or pillars, of which the central structure rises above the other two and is lit by windows on both sides of the upper part. To the characteristics of the Christian basilica also belongs the direction of the longitudinal axis, which is firmly laid down and normally goes from west to east, that is, from the entrance to the choir, which is usually a semicircular or polygonal convex termination (the apse). Historical development permits the possibility of expansion in complementary additional spaces: to the nave might be added one or two transepts, usually crossing it, but which can also be placed at its end, with an apse projecting eastwards.

Every era of mediaeval architecture interprets this basic plan differently. The Romanesque period is characterised by the principle of the addition of areas, which is conspicuous even in the external construction by adding one closed structure to another, in a way almost similar to that of 'unit' construction. In the interior, the treatment of each of its parts as independent, so that it constitutes a separate space -unit, is clearly detectable. Even the rectangular bays, each covered with its groin-vaulting, which form the sequence of the nave, looked at each for itself, have an underlying unit any character. The crossing by a transept immediately allows of three further spatial divisions: the two arms of the transept, in which independent chapels are often included, and the crossing, which can be regarded as an independent space. Naturally, where there are two transepts, these spaces are doubled; and in addition, there is the possibility of a second apse in the west, or even of a westwork with galleries that may open on to the nave only by way of comparatively small windows and may be used as meeting rooms for semi-ecclesiastical occasions. One of the consequences of the inclusion of a crypt which generally constitutes a sort of independent lower church in hall form, is that the choir, too, is separated from the nave; it is usually raised above the crypt and is reached by steps. Yet a further division of space results from the building of galleries over the aisles, which sometimes also possess altars and are intended for smaller celebrations of the mass.

In its handling of space, Gothic already distinguishes itself markedly from the Romanesque. On the one hand the new role in the service of the sermon, on the other the conception of a congregation gathered into one united body, led to a unification of the space of the cathedral – that is to say, to a fusion of the hitherto separate divisions. The bays of the nave are covered at right angles by vaulting, so that their independent character is emphasised and the follow-on of bay after bay becomes more rapid and no longer static. The transept is not now built to project so far, and through having the same height as the other vaults, the crossing no longer appears as an independent space. Supplementary chapels are now set radially upon the apse (a tendency already apparent in the Romanesque period) and thus centred upon the chancel. By the renunciation of a crypt, the chancel is now found upon the same level as the nave. The galleries over the aisles are given up; constructively, they are now less of a help than a hindrance and their disappearance prevents the splitting up of the congregation. The renunciation of the galleries and the crypt is one of the most decisive differences between the two styles; and it became general just at the moment when the Gothic appeared to become fully formed. Buildings from the transitional period often retain these separate and independent spaces. While the Romanesque preserves, in a dormant form, the space layout originally applied in the basilica and lends to the structure a concealed centrality through the doubling of transept and apse, the cathedral returns to the single-directional layout, in which the west end remains clearly a façade, an entrance and a gateway, and no longer has any rooms of its own. Similarly, the Gothic almost entirely renounces separate areas in the centre of the church, while the idea of the central structure played a great part in Romanesque.

The Spiritual Idea of the Cathedral

The meaning of the church building has also been established since early Christian times. Thus one must remember that architecture is also to be understood as one of the representative arts and has been so understood in almost all the civilisations of the world, as an epitome of the world, a representation of the cosmos or of the universe. It appears even from the writings of the church fathers that – as is frequent in oriental religions – the house of the Christian God also is understood as a representation of heaven, and that in the form of a celestial city, namely the heavenly Jerusalem, as John has described it, in his 'Revelation', 'And I saw the holy city, new Jerusalem, coming down out of heaven from God, made ready as a bride adorned for her husband.' (21,2) …'and showed me the holy city Jerusalem, coming down out of heaven from God, having the glory of God: her light was like unto a stone most precious, as it were a jasper stone, clear as crystal: having a wall great and high; having twelve gates, and at the gates twelve angels' (21, 10–12). 'And the wall of the city had twelve foundations, and on them twelve names of the twelve apostles of the Lamb' (21, 14). 'And the building of the wall thereof was jasper: and the city was pure gold, like unto pure glass!' (21, 18), etc.

These and other passages from the 'Revelation' repeatedly give prominence to similar features: the character of heaven as a city, its position suspended in air, the material of which it is built – glittering substances made up of gold and precious stones com-

Beauvais, cathedral: cross-section

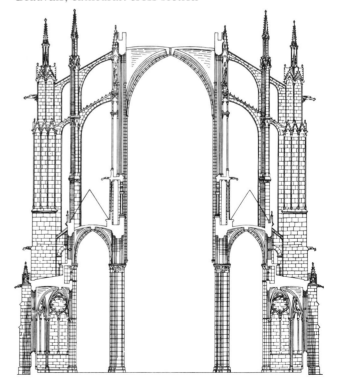

posing the walls, which, like the gates, are watched by angels.

The 'Book of Tobias' also pictures the heavenly city, the gates of which are guarded by towers whose walls are made of precious stones and whose streets are paved with white marble. The liturgy for the laying of the foundation stone and the consecration of the church established the significance of the building as a heavenly city. Already in the time of Constantine, the structure of the christian church is understood as an analogy of the city layout of late antiquity, whose origins lay in the Roman 'castrum' but whose magnificent realisation was visible in the palace of Diocletian in Spalato – a palace on the scale of a city. Thus the nave of the basilica was understood as a long, arcaded street which led from the entrance of the palace straight to the hall of audience (throne room). A cross-street traverses this main street and connects the two side doors of the construction, just as the transept of the basilica crosses the nave. The entrance to the chancel is characterised by a great, projecting arched opening – the triumphal arch. The triumphal arch motif, which occurs in Roman city architecture as a single and sometimes as a three arched opening, often with steps, finally forms also the motif of the gateway through which the faithful enter the church.

If Romanesque church architecture had moved gradually further away from this idea and had completed the transformation of the church into a heavenly citadel (since, basically, this carried on the tradition of the architectural model of the emperors, which also transformed itself in the high mediaeval period from the palace to the fortress), Gothic cathedral architecture attaches itself ever more closely to the early Christian model, just as the unification of the spatial character reached back to the days before the Romanesque. In the splendid design of the walls, also corresponding to the account of the apocalypse, and in the mosaic-decorated walls of the early Christian basilica (such as are unfortunately seldom preserved into our own day, though Ravenna shows us an example), the Gothic cathedral follows more nearly the original model of church architecture. The cathedral approaches the fundamental idea even more

Rheims, cathedral: reconstruction by Viollet-le-Duc

closely, in so far as it closes the 'heaven' above the nave with a continuous series of vaultings which in many cases were evidently painted blue and set with golden stars. In the exterior construction also, which in the early Christian basilica had lost some of its visible significance, the Gothic takes on more of the character of a city with towers and battlements.

The identification of the Gothic church building

with heaven – independent of its meaning as a heavenly city – is echoed in late Gothic painting; and here symbolism shows its capacity to function on many levels. Thus Hieronymus Bosch painted a heavenly building suspended in air. Figures from the salvation story which have entered into heaven are represented in sculpture and painting sheltered by an architectural canopy, usually in the form of a model of a church or tower. The Virgin Mary, as the Queen of Heaven, has also been identified in the liturgy with the church. Jan van Eyck places her, over life-size, in a church and makes the building her attribute (Berlin). Representations of the Annunciation are often set in churches, as for example in the painting of the Master of the Annunciation, in Aix, in the Isenheim altar, by Grünewald, and so on. Since in the view of mediaeval theology, Mary is the mediator between the old and the new Covenants, which in the pictorial representations in the cathedrals are always typologically related, the thoroughly progressive minded Gothic period brings the stylistic forms of church architecture also into symbolic use. Thus, in the Annunciation at Aix, the angel is set in an 'unmodern' frame, reminiscent of the Romanesque style and decorated with prophets and demons, while behind Mary there opens the hall of a late Gothic church.

Abbot Suger of St. Denis

The monastery church of St. Denis, near Paris, is regarded today – after the findings of Sedlmayr – as one of the most important seminal points for the development of cathedral architecture. Suger became abbot of the monastery, whose church was also the burial place of the kings of France, in 1122. Next to Bernard of Clairvaux, Suger is the most outstanding figure of his time – politically the moving power and politico-culturally the great stimulator of activity. His aims were entirely opposed to the puritanism of Bernard; and he developed from the initial stage an art of illustration in order to realise thereby a new conception of ritual imagery. For the period of his participation in the Second Crusade, 1147–49, Louis VII made Suger, in his own absence, regent of France.

So this abbot becomes ruler of France and thereby, for all practical purposes, head of the French church; and he supported the claims to dominion of the French kings with a new Carolingian ideology which also has its roots in St. Denis in so far as this was, according to legend, a residence of Charlemagne himself. Thus the cathedral, on whose façade since the time of Charlemagne the French kings had been represented, and related in confident comparison to the ancestors of Christ, symbolises the reappearance of France within the imperial tradition. The cathedral, which Suger built as a monastery church in St. Denis – and completed in an incredibly short time – became the vessel for his new conception of the meaning of the church as a 'heavenly capital', and the earthly capital of the king was symbolically related to it because part of the royal ceremonies had to take place in the cathedral in order to obtain celestial approval.

Singularly enough, Abbot Suger himself describes the building of his church in the 'Libellus de Consecratione Ecclesiae St. Dionysii' written in 1144 or 1145. From this document and from the facts ascertainable from the cathedral itself, it is evident that Abbot Suger who, through his travels, was acquainted with the church architecture of almost the whole of Europe, intended on the one hand to outdo everything possible in the architecture of his age and on the other to bind together all parts of the church building in a new spiritual order. Thus he developed a theological programme that visibly brought into play the meaning of the house of God as described by the fathers of the church – presumably in close conjunction with his friend the mystic, Hugh of St. Victor, whose meditations devote much space to the divine substance of the light. The significance of the church window in ecclesiastical architecture certainly reaches back to their common ideas.

Suger was not concerned merely with the theoretical side of the building, but knew also how to recruit to work with him the most experienced master builders, workmen, sculptors, glass-workers, goldsmiths, and mosaic-workers, and brought them from southern France, from Burgundy, and Lorraine, and even from Italy.

The Programme of the Cathedral

The cathedral is not merely a work of architecture: it is a universal collective work of art, to which all the arts have made their contribution. From this there at once arises a certain variance in our account; for without the statuary and paintings which are inseparable from the building, the picture of heaven embodied in the cathedral is not comprehensible. Their arrangement follows an iconological programme – an arrangement of images – and is bound up with the building of the church by certain relationships which later formed a more or less universally obeyed rule. In the external construction, the representation of heaven is expressed in the many-pinnacled character of the architecture and in the three great doorways in the west, north and south.

The western portals of the cathedral follow the design already apparent in the traditional Romanesque layout and show as their main motif – usually over the central entrance, in the tympanum – the representation of the Last Things, or the great court of the day of judgment. This court, with its division between good and evil, lays down the basic precondition for the admission of Man into paradise; it is also intended as a challenge to those entering the cathedral to choose, before approaching the altar, between good and evil. The late-Romanesque doorways in Conques, Moissac, and Autun, starkly emphasise the absolute character of the judgment; Christ appears in the midst of the apocalyptic scene, surrounded by angels blowing on trumpets or carrying the instruments of torment, and with the council of the four and twenty elders at hand. At Chartres, this multiplicity of figures is reduced to that of Pantocrator – of mighty stature and surrounded by the four evangelist symbols of the apocalyptic vision above the twelve apostles; but a little later, Gothic sculpture introduces the consolatory motif of dëesis into its representation of the last judgment. Certainly the judgment is still final, yet Mary and John, kneeling before the judge, lift imploring hands, pleading for mercy for sinful Man.

In addition to the representation of the judgment day, with Christ enthroned, there also belongs to the iconography of the western side the work of redemption performed by Mary. This increasing worship of the Virgin Mary – on account of which many cathedrals are dedicated to the Mother of God as 'Notre Dame', cathedrals of Our Lady – is, however, not the sole ground for the representation of Mary on the western side. There is also her significance as the opener of heaven: because of Eve, the gates of paradise were closed; now through Mary, the new Eve, they are opened once more. This close typological relationship of Eve and Mary was familiar to mediaeval typological thought, which assigned to almost every occurrence and every person in the New Testament an equivalent in the Old, in order to stress the unity of the Christian tradition and to prove that the Old Testament fulfilled itself in the New. The western side portals are therefore usually distinguished by images of Mary, enthroned under a baldaquin and surrounded by angels, and by scenes from her life; and frequently there is also a representation of the crowning of Mary, sealing in heaven the events begun by the birth of Christ on earth. In Rheims, where the glassed-in tympana do not permit of any reliefs, Mary's coronation is shown in the triangular pediment over the central western arch.

The theme of sacrosanct authority and ruling might, which is expressed in the imagery of the majesty and sublimity of Christ and Mary around the portals, is bound up in the cathedrals of France with the representatives of worldly power in the royal galleries of their upper façades. As already mentioned, they present not only the ancestral line of the French kings, but also the relationship to the Old Testament kings of the ancestors of Christ.

The portals of the transept façades on the north and south sides are also related to each other in strong antithesis. The north doorway, on the shadowy side of the building, is dedicated to the imagery of the Old Testament, most consistently in Chartres. Here there stands, in the manner traditional in images of the Mother of God, St. Anne against the central pillar, with her daughter Mary on her arm. But Mary herself is often the most important figure in the Old Testament circle of the north portal, since she herself, through

her life and through the birth of the Saviour, forms
a transition from the Old to the New Testament.
Prophets, sibyls, and kings, from the Old Testament,
the ancestors of Christ, and scenes from the Scriptures complete the circle of images from the pre-
Christian era. On the other hand, the southern doorway, on the sunny side of the cathedral, is dedicated
to the New Testament. Christ as 'sol invictor', the
new sun, stands by the central pillar, surrounded by
the apostles, saints, martyrs, and confessors.

This clear confrontation of the Old and the New
Testaments on the north and the south of the transept is apparent in the interior above all through the
rose-windows, whose stained glass shows in the centre, on the north Mary, on the south Christ, surrounded by concentric circles of – respectively – prophets,
kings and sibyls, and apostles and saints. The rose-
window over the western portal, on the other hand,
presents the Last Judgment and shows, among other
things, Christ surrounded by the four and twenty
elders of the Apocalypse. The symbolism of the round

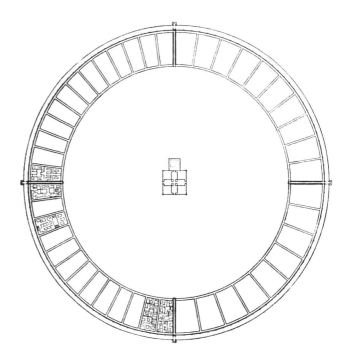

Baghdad: plan of the city in ideal form

Chartres, cathedral: west rose

window is thus many-sided. On the one hand, it may
be understood as the symbol of the sun and containing the idea of Christ as the new sun of the solar
system and the cosmos; on the other, it can be taken
as the flower itself and thus as the symbol of Mary, in
accordance with the litany of Loretto, in which Mary
is invoked as the 'rose without thorns'. Finally, the
round window can be interpreted as an abstract of
the heavenly Jerusalem, both in reference to the
ancient plan of the round city of Baghdad and in consideration of the columns set in several concentric
arcades around the central Christ or Mary.

The iconography of the remaining window-pictures,
which are themselves split up into medallions and
contain an immense wealth of scenes from biblical
or secular history, can scarcely be reconstructed
today. Yet one basic idea expressed in these windows
has been preserved: the idea of light actually trans-
forming the space inside a building whose walls seem
to consist of precious stones, as portrayed in the

Apocalypse. But it was the new system of construction for the cathedrals which first permitted the replacement of the walls with glass. Probably it was never intended, from the outset, that these hundreds of individual scenes should be contemplated each for its own sake; the deciding factor was rather the idea that the facts of the faith depicted in the windows constituted the spiritual substance of the walls, in order that those gathered in the church should be 'enlightened', since the light was of divine origin.

Mystical contemplation also heightens the significant content of the stained-glass paintings, especially with the mystics—such as Hugh of St. Victor, Albertus Magnus and Thomas Aquinas, among others—basing themselves upon neoplatonism. For them, light is the equivalent of spirit, and thus an attribute of God as well as the proof of the power of his operation. According to their understanding, light is a substance, yet it differs from other substances through its ability to penetrate glass or precious stones without splitting them. For this reason, the light penetrating the pane of glass is at the same time the symbol for the Immaculate Conception.

Above and beyond this basic idea, the iconological programme is yet more differentiated and can scarcely be described in the full wealth of the scenes it is capable of depicting. Thus we find depicted not only every conceivable scene from the Old and New Testaments, but also all the virtues and the vices, all good and evil works, all the parables of the Scriptures, and, in addition, the whole field of the theological-scientific world-picture, the seven liberal arts, the signs of the zodiac, the times of day and seasons of the year, all human employments at this time, proverbs and idioms, and the plant and animal worlds. The base areas and arches over the portals overflow with the multiplicity of subjects.

Development is not rigidly confined to this basic iconographical frame; the scheme originally conceived was varied, both at the time and later, mainly on account of local factors or in consideration of some local saint, or some other notion connecting with the original idea. Even the concentration of the figurative programme upon the portal area does not spread unchallenged. England covers the entire façade with it and often distinguishes the doorways far less. Compared with France, Germany varies the plan considerably, often preferring the arrangement of figures in the interior, perhaps as in Freiburg, where the figures of the apostles are set against the piers, or even in the founder's choir, where the strongly individual formation of the figures lends an almost scenic character to the area; whereas of course the original idea was a reminder of the eternal presence of the founders at the celebration of the mass and the example of their sacrifice. Italy transfers its assemblage of images to the pillars between the portals, and, above all, into the design of the chancel, which finds its first development in Europe here.

The basic idea of all iconography, however, is always the typological relationship between the Old and New Testaments. Thus in the entrance of the princes, in Bamberg, the apostles literally stand upon the shoulders of the prophets; and in the rood-screen there we find a similar opposition to that of the opposing portals of the cathedral—on the north side, pairs of prophets engaged in debate, and on the south, pairs of apostles. On the west façade of Orvieto, the columns on the left (north) side show images of the Old, while the right hand (south) columns display those of the New Testament. The pulpit, designed by Niccolo Pisano in the form of an octagon, bases every second pillar upon the back of a lion which holds beneath it a conquered beast. Thus a similar idea of conquest is expressed—the more as Christ, too, is often symbolised by a lion (for example, in stained glass windows). Above the eight Gothic crocket capitals, sibyls are represented, and in the spandrels between the triple arches which connect the columns, prophets and evangelists. The central column, which supports the floor of the pulpit, bears at its base the seated figures of the seven liberal arts and of philosophy. The seven reliefs of the pulpit balustrade show scenes from the passion of Christ (the way of redemption) and from the Last Judgment. They are separated by eight panels, which portray Mary and the seven virtues. The figure of an eagle, above the balustrade, symbol of the evangelist, John, and an allusion to the beginning of his gospel, 'In the beginning was the word', carries the lectern.

The Origin of the Cathedrals

Western Gothic arose in the northern French land-scapes of the Ile-de-France and the neighbouring regions such as Champagne, Normandy, and Picardy. It is founded upon a certain structure of Romanesque buildings; yet we cannot speak of an uninterrupted organic transition from the Romanesque to the Gothic. Romanesque did not take as the models

Caen, church of St. Etienne: isometric view

for its growth a few great creative structures, but developed from the beginning in sharply varied regional forms. The formative principle of the Gothic, however, was already set forth in Normandy, in the architecture of the Normans – a pure germanic root. In 1040–67, the abbey church of Jumièges was erected and a new arrangement of the walls was introduced: circular piers on the ground floor are varied by articulated, angular piers from which responds ascend to the roof-truss.

A further and decisive step in development is shown by the two principal churches in Caen, which were founded by William the Conqueror and his wife, before the attack on England. The church of St. Etienne already has responds on all its pillars, though this motif has certainly not the functional significance which it possesses in the later Gothic, where these responds continue the ribs of the vaulting and conduct its load downwards. Here in Caen, the responds have a structural character in relation to the wall, which they divide both in the plastic sense and by the play of light and shadow. To this, so to speak, pre-Gothic division of the walls through responds, however, there is added a further element in the Gothic, which helps to determine the character of the nave: the motif of the gallery over the arcades at ground level which is later to become the triforium. Within the wall-span, in Jumièges, this motif remained entirely secondary, since the two triple-arched arcade openings were unconnected and had a large space between them. In St. Etienne, however, over the ground level arcades there are wide gallery openings and above them, in the area of the windows but in front of them, a continuous arcaded corridor which is only interrupted by the portions of the wall carrying the attached shafts above the pillars of the ground floor. Here, for the first time, we find the later Gothic hollow double wall, enclosing a narrow strip of space between the outer window-pierced walls and the inner arcades. In the Trinité Church in Caen, this motif is further extended: between the arcades at ground level and the corridor before the clerestory windows yet a further simulated or apparent corridor is inserted, which emphasises still more the motif of the hollow ('thick') wall. The corridor is even prolonged through the choir and into the apse.

In the exterior building, too, substantial preparations are to be found in Normandy, in the development of the two-tower façade, at first in Jumièges, where the central portion clearly betrays its origin in the Romanesque westwork. The churches of Caen possess mighty two-tower façades and square towers above the crossing of nave and transept.

Another important root of Gothic architecture is to be found in the technique of vault building, in which an inspired return to the arts of the Romans had already begun during the Romanesque period: the Romans had already constructed groin-vaulting in service rooms of the Pantheon and in bath-houses. With the vaults, however, the structure of the walls is also changed, for it makes a difference whether a building is finished above with a flat ceiling or an open roof-truss whose weight the walls simply carry downward through perpendicular compressive forces, or whether a vault is involved which, in addition to the compression, also develops thrust forces that are exerted outwards and would therefore push apart the walls of the nave. In order to prevent this, the longitudinal walls had to be either strengthened or buttressed. In contrast to the simple type of basilica with the high nave and low side-aisles, it was the basilica with galleries above the aisles which here stood the test of time. Now the outer walls were carried considerably higher, and the space between the nave and the heightened side-aisle walls was brought into use as galleries under whose vaults hidden stone abutments supported from the side the walls of the nave.

For our immediate purpose, it matters little whether these groin-vaultings were reinforced with ribs or not. Rib vaults are first found in small and subordinate rooms such as vestibules, rooms at the foot of towers and so on, which explains their significance. The rib is not a load-bearing element of the vault but is held by the keystone of the vault. Since these ribs are heavy, they can for the time being be used only in small vaults. In the course of development, especially in the form of the galleried basilica with the stronger abutment, groined vaulting comes into general use. Yet there is still a long road to cover before the Gothic: on this road, crossribbed-vaulting

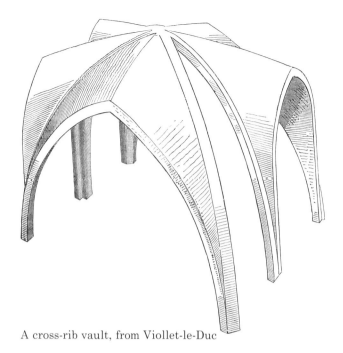

A cross-rib vault, from Viollet-le-Duc

must be developed into an independent system, self-supporting and basically variable, which in turn makes necessary new forms of buttressing. Here almost every advance takes place upon Norman or English soil, above all the divergence from the quadripartite vaulting over a rectangular ground-plan which, in the system of alternating supports had largely determined the style of Romanesque architecture. Here we find sexpartite and octopartite rib vaults arising from a square ground-plan and first and foremost those upon a right-angled ground-plan.

So there remains finally the question of the origin of the pointed arch, which has always been regarded as the conspicuous feature of Gothic architecture. The pointed arch is a flexible instrument, adaptable to the most varied forms of ground-plan. Two pointed-arch ribs crossing one another can be widely or narrowly separated, can be of different lengths or even of different widths, without thereby disturbing in the least the harmony of the whole. With the round arch, all this is impossible. Moreover, there are further static advantages: wider spaces can be covered with the pointed arch, and in addition the ratio

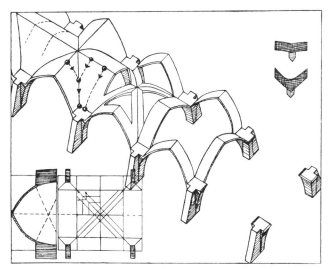

Construction of a cross-vault without ribs, showing the lines of force

of vertical stress and lateral thrust is entirely altered compared with the round arch, so that the vertical pressure is greater and the horizontal thrust less. In Burgundy, the pointed arch and the pointed cross-section for barrel-vaulting were already in use in the Romanesque period; their earliest introduction was at Cluny, already before 1100. It may well be, therefore, that it was from here that there came the technical stimulus which, through the use of the pointed arch, gave to the rib vault its new versatility.

The Construction of the Cathedrals

Despite the manifold roads leading to the Gothic system of construction, one is tempted to say that the Gothic came into being with a single, sudden stroke – the building of Abbot Suger's Cathedral of St. Denis, in St. Denis, now a rather poor suburb of Paris. The building survives only in a rudimentary form. The ambition of the unknown master-builder – perhaps too hotly fired by the theories of the light -mystics – had built upon all too small a theoretical foundation; and this soon led to the collapse of the choir, which was then rebuilt with a reinforced interior system of supports. The evidence of the ground-plan, however, and that of the rapid adoption of his

ideas in other buildings in the neighbourhood, testify to the inspired solution which he achieved: witness the interior of the cathedral of Sens, and in that of

Amiens, cathedral: system of the translucent wall, the cross-rib vaulting and the external buttresses, from Viollet-le-Duc

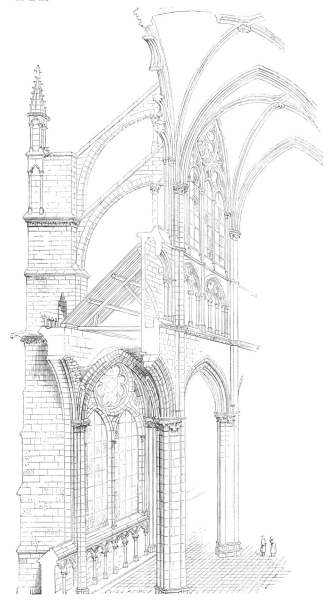

Noyon, above all the outer work of the original structure.

The constructional principle of the Gothic depends upon the almost complete relief of the exterior walls from the vertical and horizontal stresses of the arch. The ribs, which had previously been bonded into the keystones, are now so constructed that they constitute an independent cross-element which is statically balanced even without the in-filling arched surfaces, and stands of itself. The keystones are fitted into this system of cross-ribs and are carried by it. The vertical and horizontal stresses which now develop are taken almost entirely by the cross-ribs and led off to the four corner points where the vault meets the wall. In order further to control the static forces working at these four points, a new device was brought into use: upright shafts or even clusters of shafts, carry the vertical forces through the nave, by way of the piers at ground level, to the floor. The lateral thrust forces, on the other hand, are conveyed to the outer works of the building. The buttressing no longer needs to support the entire wall, as in the days of the galleried basilica, but only the four points supporting the weight of the vault. In addition, all around the outer structure tall towers are erected which project in pinnacles, and from which flying buttresses reach over to the upper wall of the nave, meeting it precisely where the thrust stresses of the vault come into play and must be taken up; these forces are led off by way of the flying buttresses and absorbed by the strong support of the abutments.

As regards the interior, this new system of construction has a special significance. What with the piers and the clusters of shafts, the walls now have no actual work to do and can thus be ignored from the constructional point of view. This constructional 'devaluation' of the walls makes it possible to replace them by openings, which may perhaps seem paradoxical but in fact exactly corresponds to the concept of the heavenly Jerusalem.

The way into the cathedral leads to the choir; and here Suger's master-builder, working upon the ideas of the founder, develops almost completely the idea of an architecture constituted entirely of light. The idea of choir-chapels – already developed in the Ro-

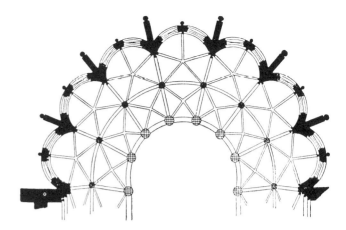

Abbey of St. Denis: plan of the choir

manesque period, especially in south and south-west France – was now to prove specially fruitful. The chapels stand in line so close to one another that more and more they tend to merge. This is particularly clear in the ground-plan of the chancel of St. Denis. Occasionally, even the side walls between the chapels are open, so that they give the impression of a double ambulatory and nothing remains of the chapel save the curved outer wall and window. Optically, this outwardly curved wall naturally offers a greater window space than if the opening between the pillars were closed in the shortest possible way. This maximum enlargement of the window surface serves especially the new idea of a mysticism of light; behind its forest of columns and pillars, the chancel will literally glow. The rays of light, coming from all sides and crossing and mingling, emphasise the shadows and with them the concrete quality of the various interior features; yet they also produce the impression – decisive for the character of the whole building – of soaring weightlessness. Without the gothic arch, however, this solution was impossible. Only the versatile and elastic system of cross-ribs in pointed arches made it possible to preserve the same ceiling height in the ambulatory and chapels and yet to cover with vaulting so many spaces, varied and many-cornered, yet giving immediately one upon the other – melting and merging one into the other.

The network of vaulting – here still subject to the severity of fundamental architectonic ideas – becomes, above all in late Gothic, an independent means of decorative expression.

The Building of a Cathedral

Almost as remarkable as the building of a cathedral is the organisation required to overcome the many practical problems in the course of its construction. Apart from anything else, the mere fact that the time required embraces several generations, during which the original conception must not be lost, makes it necessary to confine a local architectural tradition within fixed rules and principles. At the same time, those who lead the operation must not remain rigid but must avail themselves of any novelties of technique and of style which may arise during the period, in order that the building may preserve itself as a living organism and itself help to fulfil the historical growth of each generation taking part in its building.

Cologne: view of the mediaeval city and the uncompleted cathedral. Detail from a view of the city by Anton Woensam, 1531

Especially in the nineteenth century, this organisation, the masons' guild, attained an almost legendary fame. Contemporary sources of the twelfth and thirteenth centuries tell us little about its growth; but in the late mediaeval period there is much on record about its activity during the great period of cathedral building.

The organisation was directed by a master-builder, who had not only completed an apprenticeship as a stonemason but had learnt, through travels extending all over Europe, to know the most important architectural works of contemporary and historical times. He had himself taken part in the construction of foreign buildings, had assisted the master-builders in their organisational work: in his sketch-book were entered all his experiences, all new constructional forms and working apparatus which could be useful to him in his later work. Preserved in the National Library in Paris, we have half of a sketchbook by Villard de Honnecourt, a master-builder who lived in the period when the cathedral of Chartres had just been completed and those of Rheims and Amiens were still in course of building. His drawings of Chartres, Laon, Rheims, Meaux, Cambrai, Vaucelles and Lausanne, reveal to us his intensive analysis of the great buildings of his time; and we also learn from his notes that he had journeyed as far afield as Hungary.

The relationship of the master-builder to his successors was controlled by a strict craft-mystery. Only the best of the stonemasons working on the building was called in as an assistant and learnt from his superiors not only how to handle men, and the calculation and verification of the stress-factors of materials, but also how to deal with highly placed personalities and the relation between the theological origins of architectural concepts, as interpreted by their clerical masters, and their just execution. The master-builder had himself to be completely skilled in every activity carried on during the course of building. This science gathered through experience was inherited from generation to generation and found its fulfilment through the expertise of the master-builder, who alone was able to give reality to his conception.

Thus the master-builders belong to the great per-

Rheims, cathedral: design for the choir by Honnecourt

building, such as the layout of the pillars and bases, profiles of the mouldings, the roof and rafters. The most difficult work he necessarily carries out himself and the most important statues often come from his own hand. Much of the decorative work of the portals, executed by younger masons, is finished by him. He works on the drafts in his office, the 'chambre des trails', and to his immediate staff belong the foreman and the steward, who is responsible for the payment of the workmen and of the suppliers. The master-builder himself draws a fixed annual salary and is provided with a house, often with land and a vineyard, together with a horse and a servant. In case of illness or on his retirement on grounds of age, he receives a life pension. His obligation to the guild is so strict that without the agreement of his employer he may not leave the locality of his work and take up employment elsewhere – even in an auxiliary or advisory capacity.

The names of a few master-builders are known to us, especially since the end of the thirteenth century: Eudes de Montreuil under St. Louis, Raymond de Temple under Charles V; in Amiens there were Robert de Luzache, Pierre and Renaud de Corment; in Rheims, Jean d'Orbais, Jean le Loup, Gaucher de Rheims and Robert de Concy. Pierre de Montreuil became 'the prince of master-masons': he and Jean de Chelles were the most important of the known master-builders of the middle of the thirteenth century. Many of the master-builders belonged to one family and their profession was frequently inherited by sons and nephews.

With great self-confidence, these master-builders signed their works, the great cathedrals; and in this they considered themselves the heirs of the greatest legendary builder of antiquity – Daedalus, the builder of the labyrinth in the kingdom of Minos. Thus they laid out, in the floor of the western part of the nave, a great labyrinth in the centre of which they set their names. A drawing of one such labyrinth is known to us from the sketch-book of Villard de Honnecourt. The labyrinth in the cathedral of Chartres is drawn to a similar plan, enriched by an hexagonal decorative motif in the centre; here the design takes up the whole width of the nave. More advanced in its design

sonalities of their time, are often personal friends of the kings and bishops with whom they must work closely in the financing and planning of the buildings. The master-builder drafts the plans and then prepares a model, which is sanctioned by the bishop or the canons; he draws the outline and all the details of the

Chartres, cathedral: labyrinth

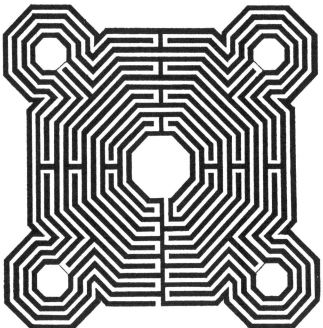

Rheims, cathedral: labyrinth

for the layout of a Gothic labyrinth is Rheims, where its outline is reminiscent of that of the Apulian imperial residence at Castel del Monte: an octagonal ground-plan, with an octagonal centre and further octagons added at four of the eight corners. In the central and outer octagons, the names of master-builders are recorded – although without dates.

We should remind ourselves again and again that the building of the cathedrals was not merely an affair of kings, princes of the church, and artists, but that a common participation of the whole people, which did not exhaust itself in idle enthusiasm, carried on the building and brought it to completion. The sources of finance which could be made available by the king, the rich nobles and merchants and the clergy, from the revenues of church lands, were far from being sufficient. Work often had to be suspended, since the payment for the masons and workmen could not be found. Then fund-gathering campaigns were organised, in addition to the already permanently established offertory boxes, and laymen formed

themselves into brotherhoods which offered their services as voluntary unpaid workers. A contemporary chronicler records that the 'Mites of the Old Women' played a considerable part in the building of the cathedral of Paris. The best account of this attitude of mind in regard to building – an attitude which was to keep an entire people in a state of excitement for almost two hundred years – is given by the writing of a contemporary, Robert de Saint-Michel, in the year 1144:

'In Chartres, in this year, one saw for the first time the faithful dragging the wagons laden with stone, wood, corn and whatever else was needed for the work on the cathedral. Its towers grew higher as though by magic. It happened thus not only here but almost everywhere in France and Normandy and elsewhere. Everywhere men humbled themselves, everywhere they did penitence and forgave their enemies. One saw men and women carrying heavy burdens through the swamps and praising God in song for the wonders which he performed before their eyes.'

Plates

Freiburg im Breisgau (Germany): the Cathedral of Our Lady

63 The right-hand jamb of the main door, in the west porch, beneath the tower. The two left-hand figures together compose a group portraying the Annunciation; then, on the right, two figures on a single base represent the Visitation. These are followed by the Synagogue, to which there corresponds the Church, upon the opposite jamb.

64 The network of vault ribs in the choir, with its large, ring-shaped keystones, is of the late Gothic period. The ribs rise out of the responds, without the intervention of capitals.

65 The ambulatory on the south side with radiating chapels. Particularly noticeable is the system of supporting wall-shafts characteristic here. The convex and concave mouldings create a delicate play of shadow.

66 The twin-windowed ambulatory chapels project in triangular form from the line of the exterior wall; a balustrade hides the roofs of the ambulatory.

67 The octagonal upper section of the single-tower façade terminates in a pierced spire. The stone lets in increasingly more light.

The Monastery of Maulbronn in Baden-Württemberg (Germany)

68 View of the west walk of the cloister. The older arcades still show the threefold division into two lancet windows and a round window with cinquefoil tracery.

69 Lower storey of the octagonal fountain-room, built on to the north walk of the cloister, opposite the monks' refectory.

70 View through the fountain-room of the west walk of the cloister. The fountain originally consisted of the flat, lower basin only; the two basins above it are a later addition.

71 Detail of the tracery of the fountain-room window.

72 The double aisled refectory of the monks, adjoining the north walk of the cloister, opposite the fountain-room. Particularly striking is the strict division of the alternating supports, as are the division of the piers by rings and the foliage capitals, barely emerged from the Romanesque tradition.

73 Corner treatment of the vault shafts in the porch of the monastery church, the oldest part of the early Gothic construction. Each element is formed in accordance with its own spatial function, its own base, its different height and alignment of the capital and the impost.

The Church of the Holy Cross in Schwäbisch-Gmünd (Germany)

74 The choir of the hall-church, with its projecting radiating chapels and the upper storey stepped back. Even from the exterior, the twofold division of the interior elevation can be recognised. The buttresses, projecting only slightly in the upper storey, form the dividing walls between the chapels in the lower storey.

75 Oblique view from the south aisle to the north wall (left) and the ambulatory (right). The light streaming in from the side windows only, softly plays on the powerful and undivided circular piers, immediately above whose capitals the ribs of the vaulting begin.

The Cistercian Church at Chorin in the Marsh of Brandenburg (Germany)

76 The western façade, with the brick-built gable towering above the nave. Articulation and decoration make full use of the scope afforded by the material.

77 View, looking west, of the nave of the monastery church. The original vaulting has collapsed; the start of the ribs is the only evidence of their former delicacy.

78 Exterior ornamentation. The preformed brick allows only the minimum scope for decoration, which must conform to strict architectonic rules. The balustrade is also made from preformed elements, whose simplicity is made to yield the greatest possible richness. According to the way one regards this, it consists of trefoils, star designs, or hexagonal wheel patterns.

◀ Plans

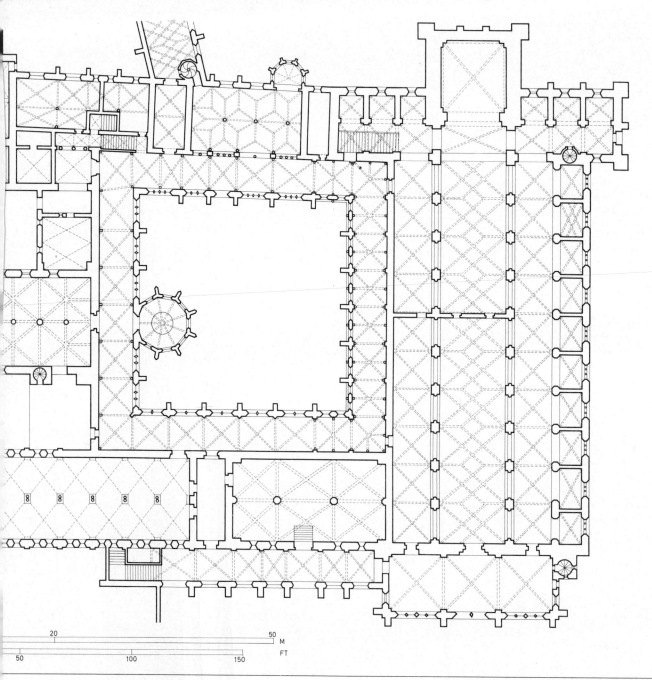

20   50
                    M
50   100   150   FT

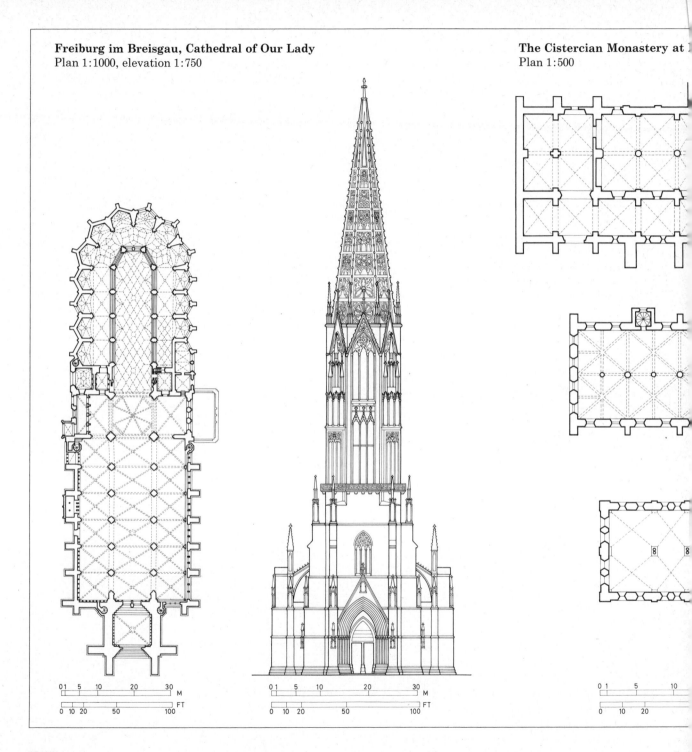

Freiburg im Breisgau, Cathedral of Our Lady
Plan 1:1000, elevation 1:750

The Cistercian Monastery at
Plan 1:500

0 1 5 10 20 30 M
0 10 20 50 100 FT

0 1 5 10 20 30 M
0 10 20 50 100 FT

0 1 5 10 20

Notes

Survey of the principal Gothic Churches of Germany

Magdeburg, Cathedral. Former imperial cathedral of the emperors Otto. Reconstruction of the choir, from 1209. Polygonal ambulatory, with chapels. 1220, choir gallery (so-called 'bishop's way') in Cistercian architectural forms. Two-part wall elevation in the nave, no open buttresses. Consecration, 1363.

Marburg, Church of St. Elizabeth. Begun in 1235, consecrated 1283. Hall church, trefoil plan in the east. Akin to Soissons in ground-plan. Two-part elevation.

Trier, Church of Our Lady. 1242–53. Important as an example of centralised construction rare in the time of Gothic. Cruciform ground-plan, with chapels in the corners formed by the cross. Basilical section, without triforium.

Strasburg, Minster. Reconstruction of the nave around the middle of the 13th century; broad proportions, through use of the old Romanesque foundation. Three-part elevation with glazed triforium, after the model of the reconstructed St. Denis. For the first time, pure clustered-column piers in place of composite piers. West façade only after 1276. 1365, completed as far as the tower platform. Middle portion then inserted, to preserve a unitary façade. In the 15th century, transformation to a single tower façade.

Cologne, Cathedral. Foundation stone laid, 1248. Consecration of the choir, 1322. Around 1350, nave and two-tower west façade begun. Building interrupted until the 19th century. Completion in accordance with the old designs, 1842–80. Connection with Amiens: ambulatory with chapels, glazed triforium. Emphasis on the vertical axis in the choir and in the five-aisled nave.

Altenberg, Cathedral. Cistercian abbey. Foundation stone laid 1255. A simple architectural unity, of magnificent proportions. Round piers in the nave. Reduced buttressing and little tracery. No tower. Large west window, filling the breadth of the façade, after 1379.

Ratisbon, the Dominican Church. Begun around 1245. Building continued until the beginning of the 14th century. Unbroken space, without transept, ending in three apses. Only slightly projecting buttresses.

Ratisbon, Cathedral. Reconstruction after 1275. Consecration of the choir around 1310. High nave arcades, broad side aisles. Two-tower façade. Glazed triforium in the choir, three apses.

Lubeck, Church of the Virgin Mary. Brick-built Gothic. Ambulatory with chapels completed in 1291, under the influence of Soissons. Nave at the beginning of the 14th century. Two-part elevation, without transept.

Vienna, Cathedral of St. Stephen. Gothic reconstruction, with partial utilisation of the Romanesque architectural elements. Consecration of the choir, 1339. Stepped hall-church, with three apses, under a single steep roof. Of the planned transept towers, only the south was completed, in 1439.

Soest, St. Mary on the Meadow ('The Meadow Church'). Nave from c. 1330, with round piers. 1351, Heinrich Parler builds the hall choir. The round piers continue into the vault without interruption. Triangular termination of the choir, combined with seven-sided termination of the ambulatory. A further development here of the hall choir of Zwettl (Austria).

Prague, Cathedral of St. Vitus. Choir begun in 1344, after the model of Narbonne, by Mathias of Arras. 1352, building continued by Peter Parler of Gmünd. Lightening of the wall by large tracery windows, then solidly arched treatment of the wall in the area of the triforium. Nave in the 19th century.

Ulm, Minster. Reconstruction from 1377, planned first of all as a hall. 1392–1419, direction of building by Ulrich von Ensingen: three-aisled basilica, without transept and with a single-tower façade. 1502–07 division of the side aisles into two twin-aisled halls. Octagon of the tower at the end of the 15th century; spire in the 19th century.

Landshut, St. Martin. Begun before 1392, completed around 1432. Main work by Hans Stethaimer. Hall-church with slender, sharply rising central piers; without transept.

Danzig, Church of the Virgin Mary. Reconstruction with basilical section, in brick-built Gothic, from the middle of the 15th century. 1387–1447, hall choir with flat termination. Around 1450, completion of the fortress-like west tower; at the end of the 15th century, transformation of the nave into a hall-church; lierne vaulting.

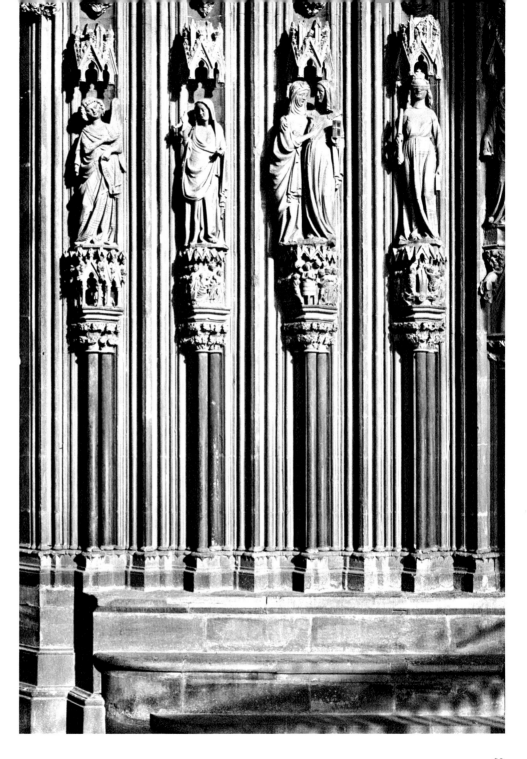

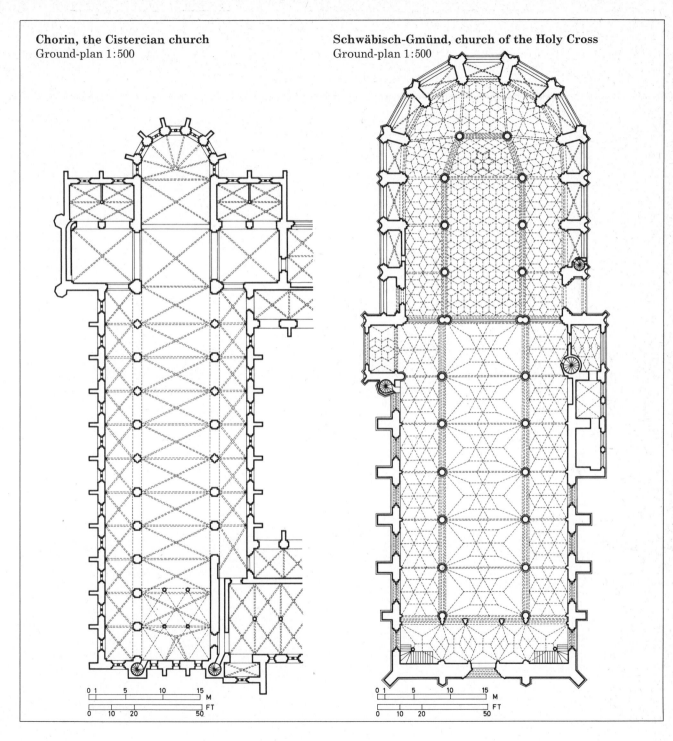

Chorin, the Cistercian church
Ground-plan 1:500

Schwäbisch-Gmünd, church of the Holy Cross
Ground-plan 1:500

79

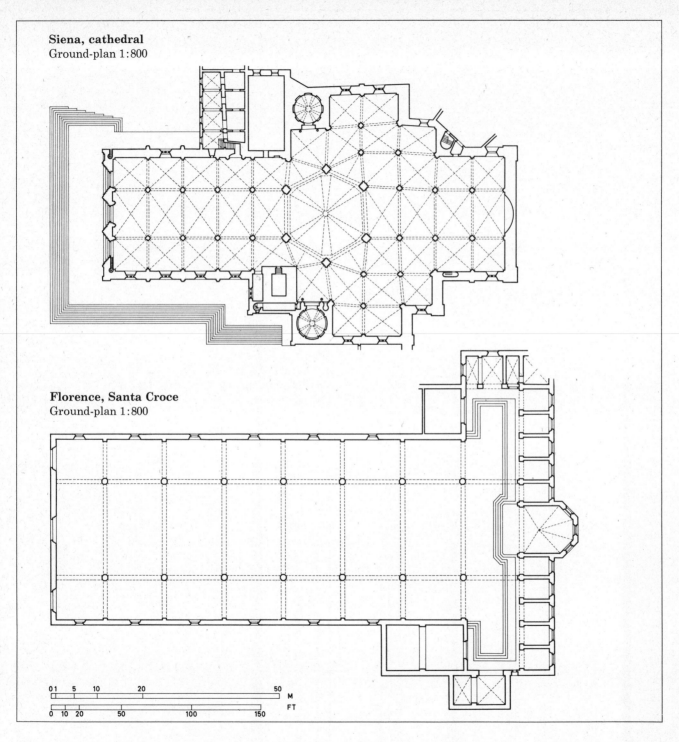

Siena, cathedral
Ground-plan 1:800

Florence, Santa Croce
Ground-plan 1:800

0 1 5 10   20   50 M
0 10 20   50   100   150 FT

3. The Model and its Variants – The Cathedral in France and in England

The Cathedral of Notre-Dame in Rheims

It was in Rheims, in the year 496, that St. Remigius baptised the Frankish king, Clovis – one of the most important stages in the conversion to Christianity of the 'heathen' German tribes, and thus also a decisive achievement in the creation of the Christian West. On the site of the present cathedral, buildings had stood one after the other for many generations; but after a fire, a new and evidently final construction was begun in 1211. For this work, Archbishop Aubri de Humbert called on one of the most experienced and, with due regard for tradition, most creative of those master-builders whose names we know – Jean d'Orbais. By the year 1241, the choir, transept and two adjacent bays of the nave had already been completed. While the building advanced from east to west, the construction of the façade was begun: between 1255 and 1291, it grew to above the height of the rose-window and in the process achieved a new treatment of the inner side, with its wall-niche figures, which is unique in the whole history of the Gothic.

In 1311, a hundred years after the building was begun, the shell was already completed; but the mediaeval walling of the towers and the addition of architectonic details continued into the fifteenth century. At the time of its first birth, Rheims was already regarded as a masterpiece of Gothic building.

From the entrance in the west, the ground-plan shows a nave, with its two side aisles, extending in the canonical number of twelve bays over the crossing into the choir. While the aisles are covered by square vaulting, the nave itself has bays of twice the breadth, roofed by vaulting of rectangular form. The basic proportions of the Romanesque system of alternating supports in relation to the breadths of the nave and the aisles are still preserved and in the third to fourth bays, where two decorative areas appear in the nave with the great labyrinth, it is as if this obsolete alternating plan were called to mind yet once more. The intimate fusion of the two-towered façade with the nave is already apparent in the ground-plan; and the exterior aspect on the west will confirm this: the first western bay, which is somewhat wider than those which follow, lies in the lower part of the façade, which gives entrance to both the nave and the aisles. The whole mighty construction rests upon comparatively slender piers, little different from the remaining supporting members of the cathedral. Only to the west do strong buttresses stand out, narrowing outwards so that the sloping jambs of the portals, on which the decorative figure-work is displayed, are formed between them.

After the ninth bay of the nave begins the crossing with the similarly threefold transept, which, however, is of comparatively narrow construction and penetrates the nave from the side to a breadth of only one bay in each case – in contrast to the transept at Chartres, with a width of two bays. The blending of the two basic lines, however, is so complete that already in the tenth bay of the nave one finds oneself in the western aisle of the transept, without having perceived, in approaching from the western doors, any sign of this crossing; only if one glances aside does the broadening, as it were, into a hall become apparent.

One cannot explain it, but looking outward from the crossing, one feels the animation of the spatial relations, for all the stark density of the individual forms. It springs, in part, from the manifold variations from one and the same spatial form, which one can clearly read from the ground-plan; while from west to east the nave continues in its original breadth, the outer bays of the transept are somewhat broader, and the main aisle of the transept is rather smaller than the nave itself and quite clearly subordinated to it. As one turns towards the choir, the spatial diversity becomes particularly clear, for – as in Chartres – the preparation for the choir begins in the transept: the bays inserted between the transept and the choir are of five aisles, though somewhat contracted in comparison with the transept, yet so arranged that, standing in the western side bays of the transept and looking eastward, this succession of spaces may give the impression of an extension of the nave. At the same time, the narrow bay preceding the choir, belongs to the two still continuing aisles on either side, while in the middle it is already part of the choir. Thus there exists here a multiplicity of spatial relations which, though in fact most strictly ordered,

conveys to the observer an impression of utter lack of design, reinforced by the fact that it is impossible from any point outside the nave to catch a glimpse of the choir, since every new angle of view vouchsafed by a walk through the cathedral meets unavoidably with the rounded surface of a pillar. Only the straight and direct road leads, visually, to the holy of holies.

Both in the interior and exterior construction, the choir is the new and miraculous work of Jean d'Orbais. The side aisles continue round it in the form of a simple ambulatory and give access to five comparatively deeply formed chapels, of which the centre one has the greatest depth. From the centre aisle, there is a free field of view between the columns of the hemi-cycle precisely to the central window of this middle chapel. Anyone who has visited French cathedrals may recognise, precisely in the structure of the choir, the multiplicity of possible solutions, using the same plan of the choir and ambulatory with chapels, and should experience what is special and characteristic here as an individual building-form. More sharply than, for example, in Chartres or Paris, these chapels are distinguished from one another and from the ambulatory, yet united in the gentle rhythm of the hemi-cycle: even the comparison in ground-plan with other solutions makes this clear. The outer mantle is neither rounded off in a schematic curve, as in Paris, nor rendered restlessly rhythmic by connections between the chapels, as in Chartres, nor divided by isolated chapels standing out individually from the general form, as in Le Mans, nor yet elongated, as in Anvers, by a projecting central chapel. Far from being understood as a negative criterion in relation to these other buildings, this should emphasise the beauty of the treatment of the choir of Rheims. In the ground-plan, strong pillars are to be found between the chapels. They encourage the supposition that the master-builder had to reckon here with highly complex static relations; and this is obvious when we consider that the entire weight of the vault covering the centre of the choir had to be carried outwards beyond the ambulatory and the row of chapels.

The outer aspect of the choir – the most ancient part of the building – shows particularly clearly the intention to achieve, in the cathedral of Rheims, an exact representations of the many-towered city of heaven. Each chapel rises from a round base, to achieve – hidden by a buttress which accompanies it almost to its full height – the transformation into a polygon. Above each of these buttresses, between the windows, an angel stands sentinel. The roofs of the chapels are hidden by a surrounding balustrade – an imaginary battlement manned by angels and demons, who seem to keep a watch on all that approaches the cathedral. Between the chapels rise apparently slender buttresses, whose real mass is cleverly hidden between the buildings themselves. These may be identified with the watch-towers of the city. Under a baldaquin upon pillars stand angels as though in sentry-boxes (pinnacles), to keep their high watch upon the city. The architect divides the burden of the choir-vault between two supporting arches, one superimposed upon the other, thus rendering possible the execution of these with a breath-taking slenderness, the outer arch being yet more slender than the inner. Yet he avoids all hazardous risks and supports these arches both in the choir and upon the intermediate pillars, yet again with a squat and powerful column. The optical effect of this is lighter than that of an angular pillar and it fulfils the same object. Thus there arises the impression that from the outer edge of the city wall, suspension bridges lead up to the stronghold of the throne room which, protected yet again by battlements, rises far above the lower quarters of the city.

This system of towers covers not only the choir for which it was designed, but also the sides and even the façade of the cathedral; yet this advanced architectural period diverges from the original picture of the cathedral as it was to appear when complete. In comparison with the design for Rheims as a seven-towered cathedral, we may observe in the present building important differences which are based not only upon a new stylistic feeling but also upon pure economy in building. In the design, whose intentional fantasy cannot be overlooked, it is possible almost to detect the traditional Romanesque principle – relinquished in later development – of the addition of parts to the building. Thus, above all, in

the execution, the tower surmounting the crossing was given up, since in the interior also the crossing itself was not to be so distinguished. In any case, the crossing tower at Rheims was conceived as without any relation to the interior and arose independently, as an open canopy above a platform. But the ends of the transept, which also appear in the design as twin-towered façades, were reduced. When the build-

Rheims, cathedral: façade

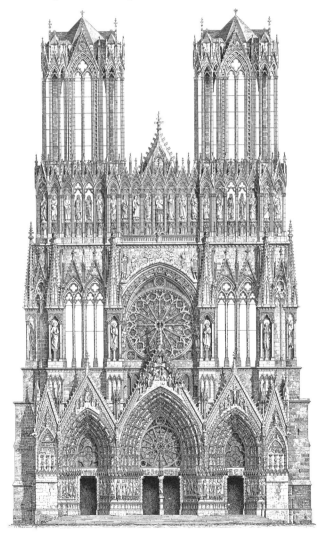

ing was first begun, the idea was still entertained of a treatment almost similar to that of the west façade, as is shown by the ground-plan of the completed building, with mighty buttresses in the lower part. But in the course of building, further construction on these lines was relinquished in favour of the dominant west façade, which now became a more important component of the exterior, as a counterweight to the treatment of the choir.

The west front, too, makes clear its close relationship to the inner space of the cathedral which lies behind it by the three portals, whose breadth is graduated according to the spaces to which they give access, by the rose beneath the vault of the nave, and the triangular fronton which repeats, above the royal gallery, the central gable over the portal. And yet in Rheims too, the façade is developed as an independent architectural entity. Even the division of the storeys, which is carried from the sides of the church inwards, undergoes an alteration conforming to the legitimate autonomy of this component. Thus the moulding above the rose lies somewhat higher, that beneath the rose somewhat lower than the corresponding moulding in the nave. On the other hand, the pinnacles are also attached to the buttresses of the façade. The lowest storey of the façade, the portal area, receives its own special significance, as against its simple purpose as a mere entrance front, from its extension into five divisions by means of the two small gables added at the sides. With the rise, in the background, of the great middle storey, with the rose and the two flanking groups of windows, the clear impression is given of a spatial build-up, step by step. Since the surface layer of this second horizontal area is to some extent hidden behind the portal gable, the impression is created that this portion of the building is suspended in the air. Its independence in space is shown above all in the lower parts of the towers, pierced with windows which allow a free view of the roofs of the side aisles, yet are not structurally concerned with these. In a manner previously unusual, the rose is not surrounded by the surface of the wall but forms part of a broad window in the shape of a pointed arch, for reasons we shall discuss when speaking of the interior of the west wall.

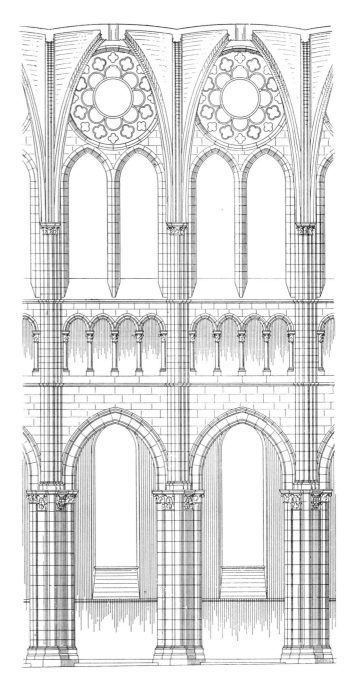

Chartres, cathedral: wall-elevation of the central aisle

As the row of pinnacles fronting the buttresses was still complete, the rise of the next storey, with its gallery of kings leading round the towers, created a similar effect to that of the division of the last storey. Since the niches, with their pyramidal crests, could plainly be seen to stand in front, the gallery of kings was clearly marked out as rising up behind them. This same effect repeats itself in the disposition of the towers, which in turn seem to mount up behind the royal gallery; and the same intention was to cause the crests of the towers to rise above the gables of the belfry level. The gable of the nave, ascending above the centre portion of the front, seems, on the contrary, not so much to rise up behind the royal gallery as to be crushed by the weight of the towers and even to sink down behind the façade. Thus, by a multiplicity of means, the total effect of the construction is achieved: all the upward-tapering members, all the climbing and striving forms, seem to contradict the massive burden of the façade, and the whole building seems to be suspended in air.

Even the interior expresses this character of an aerial structure, a city poised in air. The elevation of the walls is, as in Chartres, in three parts, with a high arcade, a triforium set against a wall, and the clerestory windows of the nave. Thus the wall does not stand for a boundary or a closure to space; rather, through its transparency, the borders of space are veiled and elusive. The impression of suspension is also achieved in large part by the contrast which exists between the slender responds, columns, and profiles of the upper portion and the strong, heavily formed, composite piers of the ground-floor arcades. The area of the capitals – here disposed for the first time at an equal height – when seen in order, effects a division, as if the upper part (with its own bases for the responds), gliding down from above, had alighted here.

In contrast to the plain circular piers of Paris and Laon, the master-builder of Chartres has attached crosswise, to each pier, four thin half columns which, on the one hand, further augment the arcade piers and on the other, make clear the function of the piers in the spatial succession both lengthwise, transversely, and in the vaulting and arches. In contrast to

Rheims, cathedral: leaf capital

Chartres, where the individual components are far more strongly differentiated than in Rheims – where everything tends strongly to merge – here in Rheims, this row of composite piers also is standardised to correspond with the round form of the whole body of the pillars.

A further and far-reaching achievement in the amalgamation of forms such as those at Chartres into a new unity is to be found in the distribution of windows in Rheims. For the first time, in Chartres, there was developed the Gothic nave window; that is to say, for the first time, a light pierced wall was created which, in its translucency, came near to being a counterpart to the ground-level arcades. In order entirely to fill such an opening, of the width of an arcade, with stained-glass pictures, the overseers at Chartres had arrived at a new window-grouping: they had placed two of the well-known lancet-form windows close together and above them – like the lancet windows, filling the entire width of an arcade – a round window, divided in the same way as the great rose windows; that is to say, with an octagonal centrepiece surrounded by alternating large and small quatrefoils to the number of sixteen in all. The system of this round window was thus still that of the pierced wall-surface. Its purpose was, together with the two lancet windows, to transform the whole window space into one single arch.

Rheims, cathedral: window tracery

As we have already remarked in connection with the rose in the west façade, the overseers at Rheims went a great deal further. They no longer thought of a wall which was to be pierced by windows, but of an opening which windows were to fill. In the great pointed arch of the window-opening, they set the same elements as in Chartres, but allowed these to merge freely into one another. Between these elements there is no longer a wall in being; the window, like the entire building, is constructed out of the members of a framework. The two lancet windows consist of the three uprights and two narrow profiled pointed arches, set upon these. Immediately above is the round window, with a six-lobed motif, while the spandrels between the lancet windows and the round window and above the round window – completing the arch of the entire opening – remain likewise open, or may be glazed. Thus is born the principle of the tracery window.

This system of unitary organisation may be seen at its fullest and clearest in the interior wall of the west façade, all the translucency and transparency of the building being concentrated here. The path from the choir to the western portal allows us to experience this phenomenon both at a distance and in immediate close-up. In the vaulted area is suspended the great west rose, completed in 1285, set in its broad pointed arch on the principle of the tracery window. The piercing of the spandrel areas in the pointed arch makes us forget, for the first time, the discrepancy of all Gothic façade roses, which contradict, by their roundness, the principle of the pointed arch; the pierced spandrels to right and left at the foot of the rose, however, emphasise the broad, horizontal support and thus lead on to the glassed-in triforium, at the same time including this as an extension in a greater window-form. The conception of the triforium as an intangible envelope is strikingly interpreted by the glazing of the rear wall. The niche motif, however, is further repeated in the large niche of the portal area, which again is inserted in the façade like a great lancet window and in addition presents a glazed tympanon over the portal, in which the great west rose is in some degree brought nearer to the people in the cathedral.

This spatial niche motif is repeated yet once more in the walls next to the entrance niche, which arch themselves divided into rows of niches, set one above the other, each holding a figure that demands and occupies its own space. The reason for this new departure remains unknown: no such treatment – apart from the single figure in its niche, traditional since Roman times – had been known before. In order to achieve unity of treatment, several niche-figures can even be linked with one another. Decorative fields, separating the rows of niches and filled below with curtains and above with leaf work corresponding in its naturalism to the late leaf-capitals, similarly absorb space and retain it. Thus, in Rheims, in every part of the building, the same principle of form is clearly to be identified and sets the standard for all Gothic architecture stemming from the Ile-de-France.

The Sainte-Chapelle in Paris

The architectural complex of today amidst which, almost hidden away, the Sainte-Chapelle may be found, had its nucleus in the Palais du Roi erected by Saint Louis in the thirteenth century.

Philip the Fair extended the palace to the Seine. When, in the sixteenth century, the king moved to his newly built palace, the Louvre, the old royal palace became, as the Palais du Parlement, the seat of the highest royal court of justice. Since the revolution it has become the Palais de Justice.

One of the chief works of French Gothic, erected in a few years between 1243 and 1248, it already betrays the revolution in general architectural thought in departure from the concept of the cathedral. By the middle of the thirteenth century, the chapel becomes the new model of architecture and there arise the buildings in Saint-Germain-des-Prés, Saint-Germain-en-Laye, Saint-Germer, the archiepiscopal chapel in Rheims, the chapel of Vincennes, and so on; and the extended chapel additions to the cathedrals are visibly increasing. This tendency to single out the chapel from the great cathedral complex, already heralds the new attitude of piety of the mystic, even if the chapel of this period, as 'capella vitrea', still clearly betrays its connection with the cathedral and in its decoration and proportion shows a royal attitude to architecture. Yet the desire for individual private devotion will in future not confine itself to the king.

Following the tradition of court and palace chapels, the Sainte-Chapelle was erected as a two-storeyed building. The less elevated lower chapel was intended for the worship of the palace staff, the high upper chamber for the king and his court. In the outer structure, the two-storeyed construction is not immediately visible. The chapel, set in an exiguous courtyard, shows itself as a tall, narrow building, on strong foundations rooted in the ground (this impression is intensified today, since the ground of the surrounding courtyard has been raised), and an upper structure contrasting somewhat with this base and having a steeply pitched roof. The relationship between the lower and upper parts thus conveys here, also in the exterior the impression of floating, which is increased by the ridge turrets added later, though this late Gothic element detracts rather from the sober plainness of the basic building. Another later addition, the western entrance-hall, which obstructs the view of the rose, also obscures the originally purer outline of the exterior. An effect of extreme and crystalline lightness is achieved in the choir and the sides by the buttresses set against the wall tapering up from the massive base pillars of the lower storey and terminating in turrets which rise up above the shoulder of the roof. The pointed gables surmounting the windows rise similarly above the roof shoulder and thus strengthen the impression of a free ascent, overcoming the ties of earth.

Certainly, the chief effect of the Sainte-Chapelle is concentrated in the interior. The usual path for visitors today, which leads from the lower church to the principal upper hall, was not originally foreseen, since the two chambers belonged to quite different social classes and had their own entrances, while the existing route is an improvisation, leading through the narrow tower staircase. Each of the two chambers was conceived as independent in itself, yet, through its part in the basic plan, subordinate to a higher general order, whose laws were, certainly, determined by the superstructure. In the lower storey, there is a low hall, with a broad central aisle, very narrow side aisles, and low-hung vaulting which determines the spatial impression. The side aisles which lead round the eastern end of the choir have no independent spatial character but are erected for constructional reasons: the arches of the chamber do not carry merely themselves, as in an ordinary hall

Paris, Sainte-Chapelle: window with pinnacled gable and balustrade

church, but also the heavy floor of the upper church and even a part of the downward thrust of its vaulting. With the exterior buttresses projecting so slightly, corresponding buttresses would have to be added in the interior. The architect avoided the resulting impression of a ponderous distribution of niches (such as we shall find later in Albi) by splitting up the buttresses, optically, into the sturdy shafts and the piers themselves, close in front of them, which, in addition, he linked with one another by means of ornamentally articulated supporting arches that conceal tie-beams. Thus this lower chamber, in spite of the stability which it had to possess as the basis of the upper church, acquired a light and translucent pattern which was emphasised by the pointed-arched arcades before the walls and by the transparent gold and blue colouring with which all the architectural components are painted.

In contrast to the powerfully squat proportions of the hall church in the lower storey, there rises above it to a great height an upper church dominated by the vast coloured surface of the windows. It has been rightly and repeatedly stated that this chamber looks like a cathedral choir that has become independent and in which a floor has been introduced at the level of the triforium. Without doubt the architectural idea behind this fifty-six foot high room is not one developed from the chapel; rather, here is merged all the experience which the master had been able to gather in the construction of the upper parts of cathedral choirs. The hall develops in a series of four bays and comes to an end in a five-sided choir. The mass is resolved above the level of the bases, into the pure framework of the piers carrying the vaulting, which are themselves split up into attached staffs and which – as we saw in the exterior – received there reinforced abutments to their full height. Precisely these sturdy responds, positioned in the interior, strengthen yet again the impression of translucency given by the hollow wall, since, together with the base level, they hold the glass windows in a second plane, disposed further outward. Thus here, too, we find, in the linking of constructional system and Gothic sense of space, an overriding unity. A blind triforium, completely merged into its decorative

Paris, Sainte-Chapelle: leaf capital

of thorns. Branches of thorn, the symbolism of rose and sun, find their climax once and for all in the great west rose, a magnificent example of Gothic flamboyant tracery from the fifteenth century.

The Cathedral of St. Cecily in Albi

The difference between the Gothic of the cathedrals of northern France and the buildings of the south and south-west is so great that it is impossible to speak of a transformation of the original Gothic type. Here we have rather an architectural thought rooted in its native landscape, for which the influence of northern France represented merely a broadening – even if very welcome – of its own artistic ideas. The south of France clearly bears the stamp of Catalan-Romanesque architecture and has a far more intense relationship to the massive quality of walls, which it has indeed no wish to deny: it possesses naturally so much light that it desires rather to shade its interiors rather than to light them.

Here in the south, too, the idea of a fortified royal castle is more familiar than that of a city protected only by stone angels. Since the Romanesque period, church architecture has played a great part in the fortification of cities. Thus Albi, built as a fortress church between 1282 and 1480 upon a hill above the river Tarn, is visible from far off, towering over a countryside which was attempting, during this period, to recover from the terrors of the Albigensian wars.

Two basic views determine the nature of this cathedral: the fortress-like character of the exterior and the closed hall of the interior. The ground-plan shows the capital F form of an extended trough; the buttresses needed for the abutment of the vaulting are drawn inward and indicated on the exterior only by a round column that exists just for visual and not for constructional reasons. There is neither a transept, to break through the longitudinal axis, nor an ambulatory, nor yet any columns or piers. The interior follows the plan of the church with wall-piers, whose system determines also the polygon of the choir; the deep space between the wall-piers is utilised for the construction of built-in chapels. Here

arcading, is set in front of the entire lower storey, which is determined by the walls themselves.

The arrangement of figures in the interior – with the twelve apostles on the engaged columns which rise up, symbolically, from the level of the bases to the window area – corresponds to the character of the chapel, which was conceived and used as an interior. Scenes of martyrdom in the arcade passages, angels with martyrs' crowns, palms and censers in the relief-filled spandrels, emphasise here the interior programme of the great passion of Christ, which was to find its culmination in the reliquary with the crown

too, the number of bays is determined by the canonical twelve; they are of exceptional breadth but of small depth and covered by ribbed cross-vaulting. Each bay is pierced by windows on either side in groups of two, one above the other – the narrow, lower window without tracery, the upper, elongated window, in contrast, having a simple tracery work consisting of a sexfoil and two trefoils, set below it, and both windows ending above in a round arch.

Between the semi-circular pilasters at the base of the interior buttresses, these windows give the effect of long narrow loopholes, well-known in southern French fortifications. The mighty west tower, copied from a fortified keep, and scarcely resembling a church tower, strongly emphasises the fortress-like character of the whole. With the exception of the scanty tracery of the high windows and the flattened lisenes of the upper termination, completed in the nineteenth century by Viollet-le-Duc, the building is without plastic decoration. The local method of building, in brick, does not permit of any subsequent working of the material. All the greater, then, is the art of the master-builder in creating, out of the small building components at his disposal, wall surfaces of such plastic impact. With extraordinary optical skill, flat surfaces are set off against round, edges are emphasised, the tower-like columns cut into the polygonal bases and give rise to curves reminiscent of the mathematics of conic sections. The love of the north for geometry is here superseded by the love of spherical geometry, which now, for its part, lends the building a crystalline impression which – even if achieved through other means – completely fulfils the spirit of the Gothic.

Similar effects, from features never before seen, are offered by the interior, the mighty depths of whose hall hold wall-strip pillars that fill the entire vertical space and deep-drawn vaulting; one is reminded of the heavily barrel-vaulted Romanesque hall-churches of the Mediterranean region. If, originally, the impression existed that it was customary in the fifteenth century to divide the space between the wall-piers horizontally into galleries above and

Albi, cathedral: window

low chapels beneath, it is here removed. Even if the walls themselves have nowhere been lightened by sham arcade grilles or similar means, but have been firmly based on the closed-wall principle, yet the transversely set wall-piers bring about an enclosure of space which even achieves something of the effect of hollowness or translucency – through quite other means than those of the north. Unfortunately, the original spatial impression of the interior has been altered not only by the later subdivision of the wall-pier niches but, after 1500, by the addition of a closed choir, on the Spanish model. This closed choir is entered through a filigree-like rood-screen, which, together with the addition to the choir and the late Gothic canopy over the main entrance on the south side, belongs to the finest small works of late Gothic decorative architecture. These external and internal additions, with their 'vesica piscis' patterns, the sweeping pointed arches, as well as their rich figure-work, form a sharp contrast to the sober functionalism of the earlier architecture. Albi is the type of a group of southern French buildings quite independent of the influence of the Ile-de-France, such as the cathedrals in Béziers, Saint-Bertrand-de-Comminges, Perpignan, Montpellier, Lodève, Marmande, Saint-Martial, and les Célestins

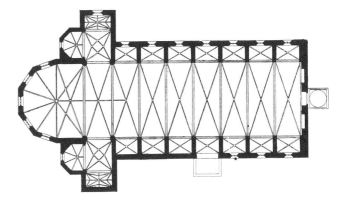

Perpignan, church of St. John: ground-plan

in Avignon, which all have the same single-nave construction.

The Jacobin Church in Toulouse

The sober fortress-like character of the cathedral of Albi corresponds not only with the special purpose of the building – which is given almost exaggerated expression by the layout of the exterior – but with the general style of southern France. This is made clear by a glance at the principal church of the Dominican order, in Toulouse – the Jacobin church, so called after the first meeting place of the Dominicans in Paris, close to the church of St. James (Jacobus) of Compostella. This building, begun in 1260 and consecrated in 1292, embodies the opposition of the mendicant orders both to the cathedrals and to their claim to be a representation of heaven. The practical, unemotional approach of the Dominicans turns the church into a functional building: its exterior, with its absence of all decoration, its simple brick structure and unpretentious architectonic organisation – almost resembling a great granary – seems almost to rebuff the onlooker; the interior is simply a community hall with a threefold purpose – for the hearing of the sermon, for the common celebration of the mass, and for the prescribed individual masses of the priests of the order. But it fell to the lot of the outstanding Dominican masterbuilder in Toulouse to give to the

Comminges, church of St. Bertrand: ground-plan

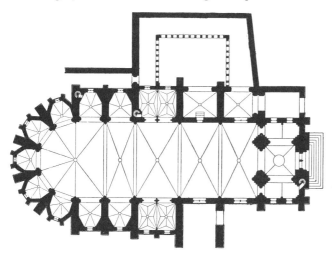

programme of this mendicant order an architectonic shape which, without further ado, could match the artistic greatness of the cathedrals not through decoration but in the consummate radiance of space, and created a house of God whose effect is made by architecture alone – in enclosed and organised space.

The ground-plan and exterior clearly show the system of the wall-pier church which we have already met in Albi, but with an important difference: here the piers are set against the exterior wall – though on the south side the walls are pierced in the lower storey and chapels have been built between all the piers; and on the north side there are two chapels

Toulouse, the Jacobin church: window

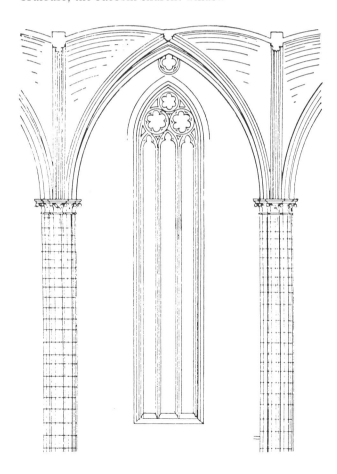

and an entrance hall to the transept aisle. In the ground-floor area of these chapels, therefore, the piers are found in the interior; in the area of the narrow high windows, they are outside. A built-up reinforcing arch, which provides an additional counter to the side thrust of the vaulting, connects the exterior piers with one another, so that here, above the comparatively smooth storey bearing the chapels, rises a spacious broad pattern of niches. This disposition of the walls has, of course, exactly the opposite effect in the interior: there the chapels alongside the nave form deep roomy niches, while above, the area of the windows preserves its internal smoothness. The system of chapels is carried on round the choir also, in accordance with the cathedrals' system of chapels radiating from the choir; the interior arrangement, however, is scarcely influenced by the chapels set more deeply onto the choir, which only appear more clearly in the exterior. The decisive factor for the impression of the interior wall remains its effect of space in the chapel storey only; yet, as a whole, of the limitation of space, in which the windows – originally constructed in grisaille – played their part.

This interior space receives special emphasis as the place of sacred ceremonies. It is a large, unitary hall-space, with central supporting pillars; it cannot be properly described as twin-aisled, since the two aisles which result from the central pillars are entirely subordinated to the spatial unity of the whole and do not lead on to any separate terminations but are reunited in the choir. The height of twenty-two metres, to which these unjointed circular piers – corresponding to the simple, smooth side walls – rise up, bearing above rib-vaults built of brick, certainly oversteps purely functional needs: the artistic purpose of the architect, taking precedence over utilitarian factors, is immediately apparent in the spatial proportions. And not only here, but above all in the central position of distinction given to the choir itself, in which also a concept of cathedral architecture – latent centrality – finds a modified expression. The centre of this choir is not, as in the cathedrals, a space, but a circular pier – the last in the row of central piers by which the twin aisles are led back into their common choir. It differs scarcely at all from the preceding supports but is set slightly further away and bears a mighty, spreading, fan-shaped stone vault of an unexpected beauty of design. In it unite the square rib-vaults of the two aisles – which likewise were not characterised by any division into bays (as in the cathedrals) but have rather the character of a soaring, vaulted roof coming together in the unitary principal chamber, which determines the nature of the entire church. Thus, this area around the pillar which carries the fan-vaulting is known among the people as the 'Palmier', or palm tree – a reflection of what is expressed by the room as a whole. This effect, however, was due to the Gothic pointed-arched cross-vaulting, which first made possible this asymmetrical over-arching of the choir and at the same time, the organic transition from the square vaulting of the nave to the fan vault.

The spirit of this chamber, whose distant forerunners may be found in secular halls, both meeting places and store-rooms, could not be gathered from rows of statues between glass windows or wall-frescoes, but is entirely the result of the reforming ideas of the mendicant orders, sober reflections upon the meaning of the house of God as the gathering place of the community. The twofold division of the entire space bound together priest and layman more closely than heretofore, when in monastery churches or in the cathedrals themselves a strict division between the clergy and the lay had been brought about by a rood-screen. In Toulouse, the northern part of the church with its entry from the cloister, was reserved for the monks, while the southern part, which is accessible from the town through its own entrance in the west, was at the disposal of the community. Both sections, however, prayed together in view of the same chancel.

It is in keeping with the character of the hall that it is not unconditionally bound to a fixed directional system – in contrast to the cathedral, based on the basilica, whose aisles lead up to the choir. Since in the divine service of the Dominican order, the sermon played a special part and the pulpit was built in the middle of the north wall – that is, above the exit of the monks into the cloister. The liturgical rule which prescribes for all clergy of the order the daily celebration of mass and which therefore demands, in monastery churches, several chapels and altars, is also newly interpreted here. These altars and chapels are usually disposed in the area behind the rood-screen, in widely projecting transepts (in southern France, rather as in St. Sernin, in Toulouse, or in Conques) and have thus their own part of the building, separated from the communal space. In the Jacobin church, these chapels, being built between the piers, are closely bound up with the main body of the nave and visually subordinated to it.

Exemplary as was the building of this church, its effect in the region nearby was small. Rather is its influence more apparent in other geographical regions, above all in southern Germany where, in the fourteenth and fifteenth centuries, hall churches arose whose architects may have known Toulouse, understood it, and adapted it to their own purposes.

The English Cathedral: Wells

In the building of European cathedrals, England, on many grounds, is the closest to France: in the first place because the Norman origin of the cathedrals also influenced the church architecture of England after the Norman Conquest; in the second because the claims of the kings of England were in rivalry with those of France and much of the conflict between their policies was fought out upon common ground. Nevertheless, the cathedrals of England differ from those of France in important respects, above all in their far stronger adherence to the Norman tradition and in the manifold spatial elements developed in their architecture. While the French cathedrals rapidly advanced to the realisation of spatial unity, English cathedral architecture maintained, to the end of the Gothic period, the traditional additive principle, with surprising successions of architectural complexes fully independent in themselves and only loosely connected to the main structure.

The west façade of Wells, with its strongly prominent buttresses, is broader than the cathedral itself. It is true that here, as in France, each nave has its own portal, but the towers do not rise from the side-aisle entrances, being positioned as it were 'beside' the cathedral. Thus the west façade appears as a broad theatrical setting, its monumental quality accentuated by the neighbouring low building of the chapter house, by its side, and by the wide expanse of grass in front, from which the cathedral rises. This latter, also, is characteristic of English cathedrals, which were not built, as in France, in the midst of a piled-up confusion of houses, but were erected outside the town upon their own ground. This broad disposition holds also a clear tendency towards an upward surge, a suspended equilibrium, which would have been even more apparent had the towers been completed. This appearance is achieved here by the marked elevation above the lower storey – the basic, earthbound area into which the portals are set – in complete contrast to the portals of the French cathedrals, conspicuous with an array of statuary that was entirely alien to the English founders and master-builders. The entire façade above the ground level is built up on the principle of the translucent wall-formation; the wall proper is hidden by a dense network of arcades bounded by gables which appear, despite their fragility, to carry one storey upon another. In the upper areas, removed from direct view, and especially upon the buttresses, these arcades contain figures of kings and saints.

The high walls between the buttresses are divided by tall, narrow arcades which, in direct contrast to the many-storeyed division of the buttresses, give an impression of light and soaring. If one approaches the central façade from the west, the significance of its broad layout – and that of almost every other English Gothic cathedral – becomes comprehensible: the western towers are so widely separated in order to give, between them, a harmonious and undistorted view of the tower over the transept-crossing which – in yet another inheritance from Romanesque tradition and contrast with continental Gothic – is a characteristic of almost all English cathedrals. No photograph of the west façade can do justice to the spatial impression – so important to the general effect – whereby the relationship of the two towers of the façade to the tower of the crossing corresponds to the division of the façade itself through its prominent buttresses. The greater part of this façade was erected in 1220–39, the upper part of the uncompleted towers – more sober and functional in its design – followed in the fourteenth and fifteenth centuries; and the right-hand, southern tower, of 1367–86 stands out with its ascetic treatment, typical of the fourteenth century, in contrast with the more richly decorated northern tower of the fifteenth century (1407–24), with its canopied figures in niches upon the buttresses. The ogival arcades penetrating into view in the northern tower as seen from the side – that is to say, in the older part – carries on into the architectonic organisation of this period the motif of overlapping forms, already well-known from Carolingian manuscript illuminations.

In cross-section like the basilica, in the three-storeyed division of the lateral elevation, the nave of the English cathedral follows the French model. Here too, however, there is no merging of the parts into a deeply-felt unity, for the separateness of every architectural element is stressed. This is true for the spatially creative piers of the arcade, which are formed in Wells of twenty-four differently rounded responds, applied to the columns of the nave, which support the arches from the impost-block; it is true for the ogival openings of the triforium, which does not appear as a continuous passage behind a line of arcades but as a horizontal row of independently constituted openings, with richly decorated jambs; finally, it is true, too, for the deeply descending vaults, whose plastic decoration thus appears far more prominent than in France.

There arises in the nave a further impression, of decisive importance, through the independent significance of the horizontal lines. No such intimate merging of the horizontal and vertical takes place here as in France, where it finds expression in the division into bays in which the responds of the vaulting reach down through the composite piers to the floor; here the three divisions of the elevation – arcades, triforium and clerestory – are underlined solely in the horizontal sense. One has almost the impression that the vertical relationship between the parts is not binding and that the horizontals might be displaced in their own plane without serious effect. Doubtless we have here a memory of the architecture of the

early Christian basilicas. It is specially remarkable that none of the numerous responds of the ground-level piers contribute to the support of the vault.

In addition to all this, there is a linear, almost graphic element which helps to determine the character of the interior. Since all the arches are divided by sharply undercut profiles, giving the plain wall surfaces in the spandrels an even flatter effect, the whole gives the impression of a decorative linearity, here not in contrast but in precise concord with the pervasive plasticity of the interior space. This linear aspect, characteristic of all English Gothic, finds its culmination in the flying buttresses of the crossing piers, which support the tower rising above it. This treatment, peculiar to Wells, was originally not foreseen. After the tower was in danger of collapse, these supports were added in 1338.

The ground-plan makes clear that the choir, following upon the transept and the crossing, is again constituted as an independent church. In the choir we find the typical addition of a closed space – such as we also find subsequently built into the cathedral of Albi – reserved for the members of the chapter. Still further to the east we find the lateral addition of two chapels, resembling a second and smaller transept, such as actually exists in other English cathedrals, as in Canterbury, Salisbury, and Lincoln. In the east adjoining it is the sanctuary with its widely projecting central Lady Chapel. The whole represents a manifold spatial division which is designed to serve the rituals of the English liturgy. This sanctuary replaces the polygonal ambulatory customary on the continent. Here, too, a photograph can scarcely reproduce the actual impression of spatial complexity. If one looks eastward from the sanctuary, through the charmingly interweaving vaulting at the sides one sees, at ground level the plain window in the east wall of the Lady Chapel; above it, however, on a level much nearer to the observer and above a wall containing the figures of saints in niches, there is visible the high, east window of the real apse, which is broken through at the lower storey, in considerable depth, by the Lady Chapel. With absolute consist-

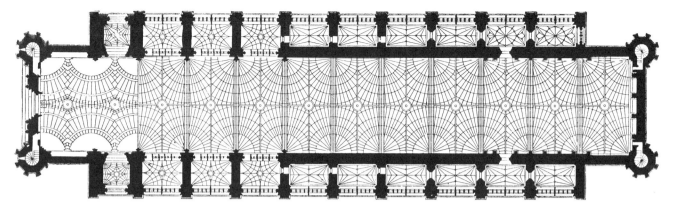

Cambridge, King's College chapel: plan

ency, the spatial and linear values – the latter prominent above in the complete covering of the sanctuary walls with tracery – are brought together in harmonious concord.

Outside the ground-plan itself, the English cathedral usually receives further additions which convert its complex structure into what is really an independent settlement. At the western end, on the south side, there is an extensive cloister with an inner courtyard about 60 yards by 40. It is bordered by the bishop's Palace, set in the midst of a beautiful park. To the north, alongside the choir, stands an octagonal two-storeyed chapter house, with a gateway nearby leading to a row of clerical dwellings, 'Vicar's Close'. Thus the English cathedral has a far more marked appearance of independence, a residence, in accordance with the idea – far more strongly developed here, since the country became Christian – of a national church, independent of Rome.

Westminster Abbey: The Chapel of Henry VII

English Gothic, like French, changes from the cathedral to the chapel, but in England the development begins considerably later and is not completed until the second half of the fifteenth century. If one was tempted, in reference to the Sainte-Chapelle, in Paris, to say that the choir became independent, it is far more justifiable, in England, to speak of a developing autonomy of the central choir-chapel; the more so since these choir-chapels – even when set against the cathedral itself as a whole – have acquired their own far more independent and spatially autonomous form. The chapel of Henry VII is of this type. It was built on to the choir of Westminster Abbey in 1503–19, but on such a scale that in ground-plan it appears almost larger than the Abbey itself. With King's College Chapel, Cambridge, this chapel is probably the most important manifestation of English late Gothic, with its typical tendency to visible spatial unity in place of the earlier subdivision of large spaces. The unity of the entire conception is emphasised by the decorative latticework that covers the walls, rises up to and through the vaulting, and seems to strive to return to earth, as though petrified in the midst of its slow-flowing movement.

Plates

Siena: the Cathedral

101 South side of the cathedral. The elongated ground-plan, with the central dome, is clearly observable from the exterior. The western façade overtops the nave behind it. Although contained within the complex, the tower is conceived as an independent element.

102 View into the octagon of the central dome. The round arches of the nave are still in accord with the long-lasting Romanesque tradition. The small columns in the drum of the dome nevertheless lighten the wall which is reminiscent of a triforium.

103 A pier of the nave, rising to a round arch.

104 View into the top of the dome, which rises from an octagonal base. Five coffered rings ascend, after the model of the Roman Pantheon, to the summit.

Florence: Santa Croce

105 View of the south wall, taken from the Piazzale Michel-angelo, giving a striking impression of the remarkable length of the building. Seen from below, the gable fronts conceal the roofs of the side aisle. The tower is a later addition.

106– View from the south transept of the north wall of
107 the nave. The hall-like breadth and the wide arcade openings determine the spatial impression, though at the same time the wall is emphasised as a boundary of space.

107 View looking east into the open roof-truss.

The Cloister of Batalha (Portugal)

108 View of the great central court, with the surrounding cloister buildings.

109 A walk of the cloister. Immediately remarkable are the strict articulation, the emphasis on the surrounding walls and the heavy vaulting. Obviously aimed at is an extreme contrast with the exterior view.

110 South side of the cloister, with the church rising above it. The architectural ensemble is one of extreme richness – a filigree screen of decorative features behind which the real Gothic structure is hidden. The change of axis between the broad arches of the cloister arcades and the more steeply rising windows of the church creates an effective contrast.

111 (A) Tracery window. (B) Detail from the south side of the cloister.

Wells: the Cathedral

112 The west façade of the cathedral. The portal area is given far less importance than in the French cathedrals. The sculptural programme extends over the entire width and height. The towers seem added at the sides and thus reinforce the strongly vertical lines.

113 Network of ribs in the vaulting of the choir.

114 The nave is built up in three storeys, like those of the French cathedrals, but with important differences: each storey constitutes a purely horizontal alignment and vertical lines are almost entirely lacking. The later, monumental buttress of the crossing-tower is unique in Gothic architecture and supports a triumphal cross, which faces towards the nave.

115 The entry to the Lady Chapel constitutes a continuation of the choir, but is lower in height.

116 Star-shaped lierne vaulting in the chapter house.

Westminster Abbey, the Chapel of Henry VII

117 The south side of the chapel, which is built on to Westminster Abbey. It belongs to the most richly ornamented buildings of the perpendicular style.

118 Detail of the exterior articulation.

119 Fan vaulting with pendant keystones in the chapel – an extreme achievement of the perpendicular style.

120 View of the fan vaulting and of the windows with their triangular projections.

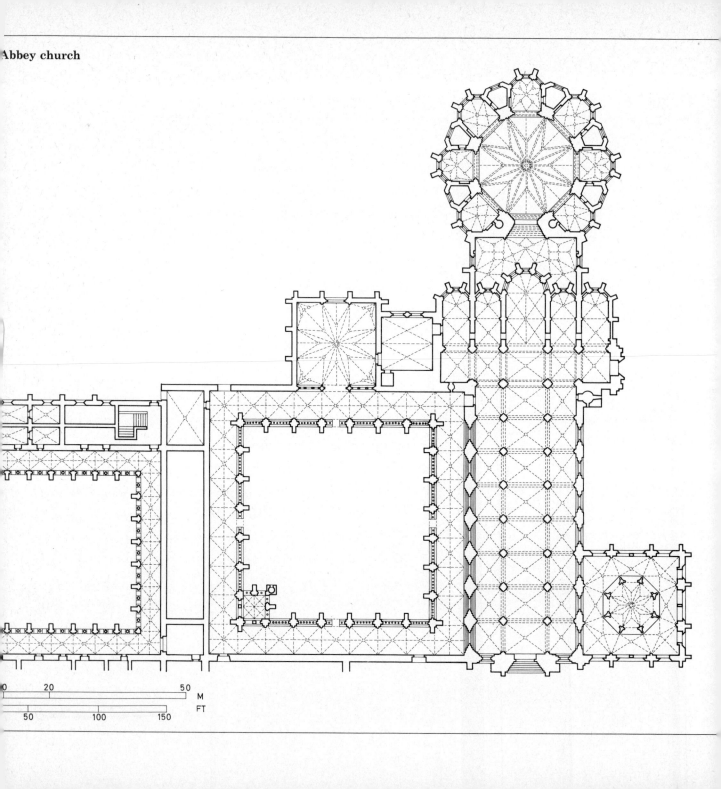

Abbey church

20 50 M

FT

50 100 150

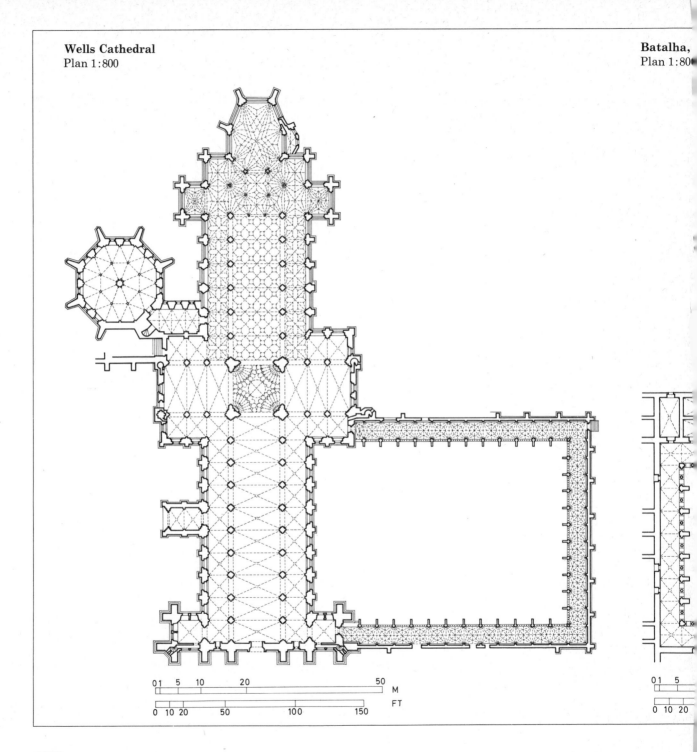

Wells Cathedral
Plan 1:800

Batalha,
Plan 1:80

0 1   5   10   20   50
└───┘ M

0 10 20   50   100   150
└──────────────────────────────────────┘ FT

0 1   5
└──────┘

0 10 20

Notes

Survey of the principal Gothic Cathedrals of England

Canterbury, Christchurch Cathedral. Romanesque, early Gothic and late Gothic portions. Begun 1067, consecrated 1130. Burnt 1174. Reconstruction from 1175, by William de Sens and his successor, William the Englishman 1179–84. Retention of the Romanesque external walls of the choir and apse. Round and pointed arches used in contiguity. Eastern transept and sanctuary completed 1179. Extension of choir and eastern chapel for the shrine of St. Thomas à Becket. Reconstruction of nave and western transept begun in 1378. Crossing-tower with fan vaulting c. 1495–1503. Unusually low clerestory windows; uniform articulation. Lierne vaulting.

Ely, Cathedral of the Trinity. Romanesque structure begun 1083, nave completed in 1180. Under Bishop Eustace, 1197–1215, early Gothic westwork before west tower; from 1234, rebuilding of the presbytery. 1322, collapse of the crossing-tower, construction of an octagon the full breadth of the nave, 1342. Fan ribs and dome structure of wood. 1321–49, addition of the Lady Chapel as single-aisled hall-area of five bays, with fan-vaulting.

Winchester, Cathedral of the Trinity. Of the Romanesque structure begun in 1079, the crypt, the north transept and the south wing are still preserved, together with the Romanesque core of the south side-aisle walls and piers. 1189–1202 wide, hall-like retro-choir, with rectangular Lady Chapel. Transformation of the choir, about 1320. Gothic nave from the middle of the 14th to the middle of the 15th centuries. Transformation of the choir aisles and the early Gothic Lady Chapel beginning of 16th century. Addition of lierne vaulting. Gothic fan-vaulting in the crossing from 1635.

Salisbury, Cathedral of St. Mary. Construction completed in the period 1220–60. Three-storeyed building with two transepts. View throughout the whole length of seventeen bays. Sanctuary with projecting Lady Chapel. Octagonal chapter house, with slender central column, built on to the south cloister, to the east. West façade articulated by low corner towers and by projecting buttresses and covered with figures in ogival niches.

Exeter, Cathedral of St. Peter. The new building, from 1224, included remains of its Norman-Romanesque predecessor. Choir and nave follow the dimensions of the Romanesque cathedral. Three-part elevation with low-set fan-vaulting, continuous longitudinal ribs. Rectangular chapter house, 1270–80.

Wells, Cathedral of St. Andrew. (See text pp. 93–6.)

Gloucester, Cathedral of the Trinity. Surviving remains of the Norman-Romanesque structure of 1089 are the nave (rib-vaulting about 1240), crypt, ambulatory with galleries and remains of walls in the transepts and the choir. Reconstructions: south transept, east and west walls, 1318–29, interior 1331–37; north crossing and transept and choir 1337–77. Thin lattice work set before the Romanesque arched openings in the choir. Lightening of the flat east wall into a mesh of stonework. Adjoining Lady Chapel completed 1472–99. West façade with large window and south transept portal, 1421–37. Cloister on north side, with fan-vaulting (east walk 1351–77, remainder 1381–1412).

Worcester, Cathedral of Christ and Our Lady. Gothic reconstruction after 1218 (east choir). Nave after 1317. Nave vaulting 1377. Crossing tower, 1358–74. In the 14th century, transformation of most of the surviving Romanesque portions into Perpendicular style.

Lichfield, Cathedral of St. Mary and St. Chad. Three bays west of the choir and south transept about 1220. North transept about 1240, nave after 1250, façade from 1280. Sanctuary and Lady Chapel completed towards middle of the 14th century.

Lincoln, Cathedral of St. Mary. Gothic rebuilding, with retention of the Norman-Romanesque portions from 1192, including the eastern transept. Crossing piers reinforced after 1239. Core of the façade and lower portion of the towers, about 1150. Broadly disposed upper portions, in high Gothic, about 1220–30; simultaneously the side portals and porches. 'Angel choir', richly carved.

York, Cathedral of St. Peter. Romanesque crypt preserved. Gothic reconstruction on the old foundations, beginning with southern wing of transept 1230–c. 1241; north wing 1341–60, with five high, narrow lancet windows. Nave 1291–1324. Triforium in five parts, forming the base of the high windows. Sanctuary with double wall, 1361–70. In the eastern half, the windows are on the interior, and on the exterior a framework of tracery; in the west half, the reverse.

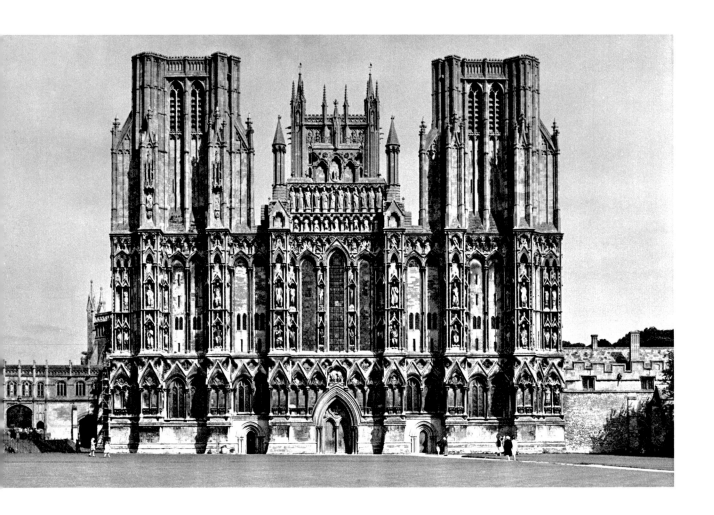

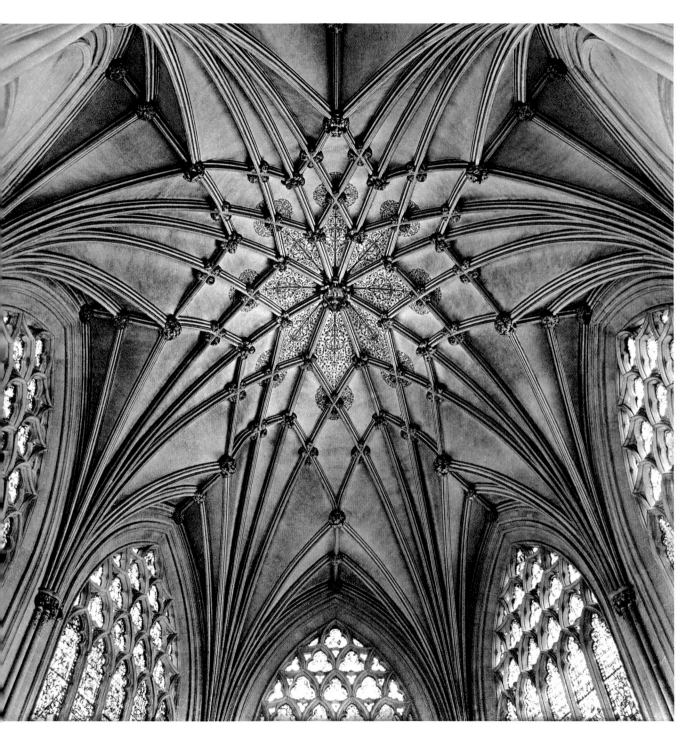

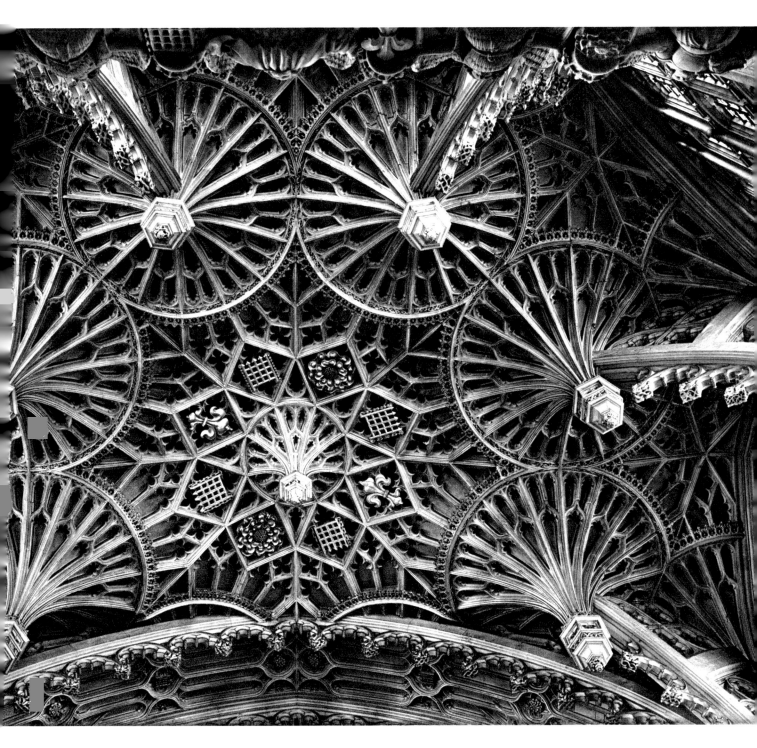

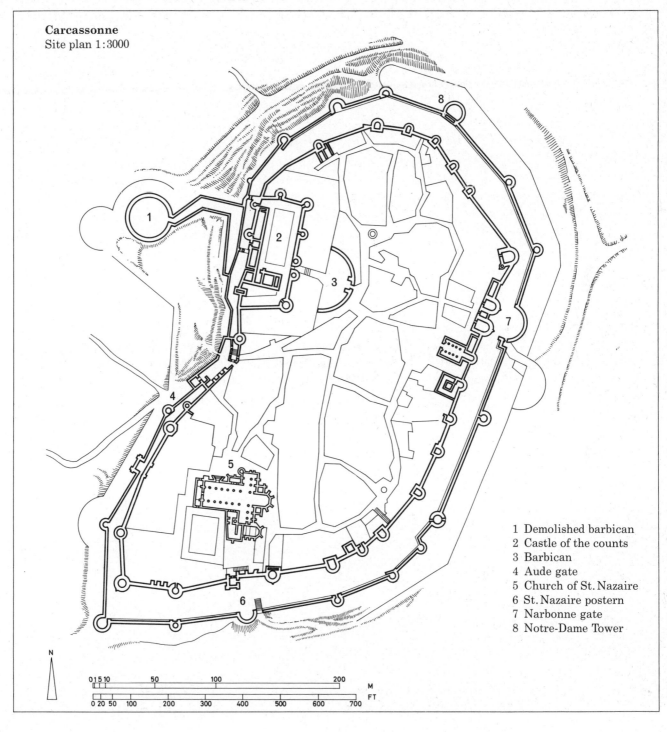

Carcassonne
Site plan 1:3000

1 Demolished barbican
2 Castle of the counts
3 Barbican
4 Aude gate
5 Church of St. Nazaire
6 St. Nazaire postern
7 Narbonne gate
8 Notre-Dame Tower

N

0 1 5 10   50   100   200   M
0 20 50 100 200 300 400 500 600 700 FT

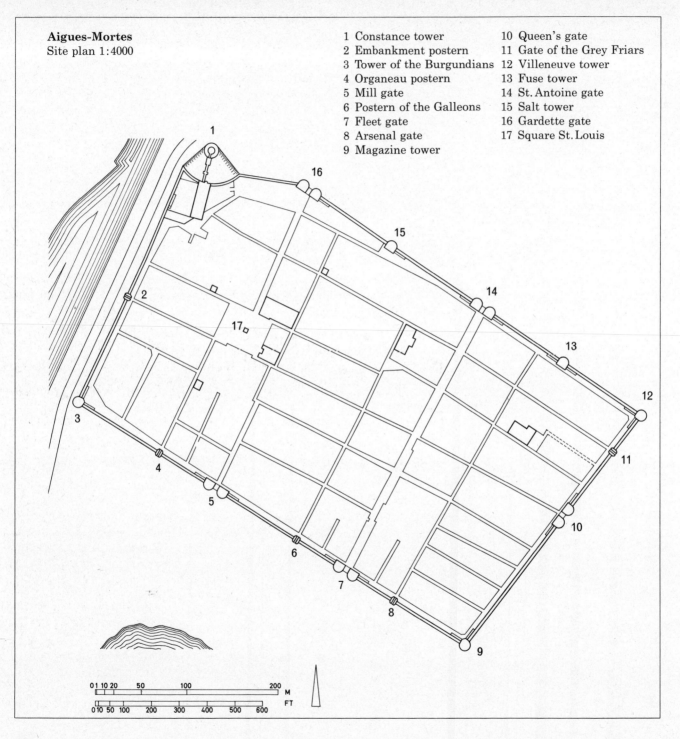

Aigues-Mortes
Site plan 1:4000

1 Constance tower
2 Embankment postern
3 Tower of the Burgundians
4 Organeau postern
5 Mill gate
6 Postern of the Galleons
7 Fleet gate
8 Arsenal gate
9 Magazine tower
10 Queen's gate
11 Gate of the Grey Friars
12 Villeneuve tower
13 Fuse tower
14 St. Antoine gate
15 Salt tower
16 Gardette gate
17 Square St. Louis

0 1 10 20   50   100   200 M
0 10 50 100 200 300 400 500 600 FT

4. The Spread of Gothic into Germany, Italy and Spain

Gothic in Germany

As was explained in the first chapter, close political relations existed between Germany and France. The king of France once saved the German Emperor's throne for him. But they were also rivals and the mediaeval German Empire as the embodiment of western culture was succeeded by the mediaeval French kingdom. If we may see in the spread of French Gothic the claims of the new statesmanship clearly mirrored; so too, we may, if so inclined, find reflected in the clinging of German architecture to the forms which had grown up with the Empire, a continued insistence on the demands bound up with it. In fact, it is only at a very late stage that Gothic begins to exert an influence upon German architecture: while in France, around the year 1200, the classic cathedrals are already in course of building, there arise simultaneously in Cologne, Mainz and Worms, new chancel buildings of a purely Romanesque character, whose building extends at least into the second quarter of the century and sometimes as far as the middle. The first church building on the Gothic plan, with the choir and ambulatory and its associated chapels and a two-towered west façade, was built in Magdeburg by Archbishop Albrecht, who had studied in Paris and knew the Gothic from the land of its birth.

It is not difficult to observe in German Gothic cathedrals clearly marked differences from their French examples. The unifying tendency of French architecture is just as alien to the German feeling for form as is the idea of the greatest possible piercing and lightening of the mass of the structure. Thus, in the German churches, the individual components are more strongly set off against one another, almost balanced in harmony with one another as in the Romanesque (rather as in our example in Freiburg). In general, too, the periods of the building operation are more strongly differentiated: a master builder newly called to the work did not follow as a matter of course the plans of his predecessor, but attempted to carry on the work in harmony with what already existed, while expressing his own ideas.

In the same way, there is in Germany a pronounced feeling for the solidity and mass of walls, in contrast to the French tendency to pierce them and lighten them: the wall as the boundary of space is here not denied but emphasised and its mass made visible by plastic conformation in depth. Accordingly, in the interior, the wall-piercing triforium is usually omitted and the closed wall area between the ground-floor arcades and the high windows emphasised. The buttressing of the exterior also is never so much resolved into its constructional parts as in France, but always grouped in compact blocks subordinated to an architectural concept.

A characteristic feature of German building is the treatment of façades rather as independent elements of the building than as stages on a road leading swiftly on to the choir. Here we may see the influence of the long tradition of the Romanesque westwork, which found its counterweight in the choir and thus expressed a tendency to latent centrality. Thus, the single-tower façades of Freiburg, Strasburg, Ulm, Constance, and Berne, or the two-tower façades of Magdeburg or Cologne, have the plastic weight and impact of earlier westworks designed as a counterweight to the choir. Almost always where we find departures from these German practices and leanings towards the French, further connections with France can also be traced. The most important steps towards the form-concepts of western architecture, however, were taken by the monastic orders, with the reduced architectural programme through which they reinforced their reforming ideas, in contrast to the artistic profusion of the cathedrals; and foremost among these were those of Cluny and later, the Cistercians.

The Cathedral of Our Lady in Freiburg im Breisgau

The ground-plan and the general view of the exterior of Freiburg Cathedral make clear on the one hand the harmonious unity of the structure, while on the other stressing that this unity is made up of a number of very different parts. The three centuries that saw the growth of the building have stamped it with the marks of very different conceptions of architectural style. From the first, the decisive fact is that the cathedral was not erected as that of a bishopric, since

Freiburg belonged to the bishopric of Constance until 1827, when the bishop's seat was transferred here. Thus the building was erected as a simple town parish church; but it was built by a proud middle class. The building was begun around the end of the twelfth century or the beginning of the thirteenth, and was connected with the cathedral of Basle, founded in 1185; and indeed, judging by the similarity of many of the details, it was executed by the same building force.

From this first phase of construction, in which an earlier Romanesque building was to be gradually replaced, there survive the late Romanesque portions of the transept and the so-called weathercock towers above them. Together with the crossing tower, these were intended in the original plan to constitute the eastern tower group. There also existed at this time a five-sided, closed sanctuary, but with the reconstruction of the nave this was later removed. These late Romanesque elements today throw a certain revealing light on the originally intended dimensions of the church, which was designed to be far smaller than the later Gothic construction. The transept was indeed, like its example in Basle, 'compressed', which is to say that it projected only slightly; the Gothic continuation, however, included it completely in the alignment of the side walls, so that in the ground-plan it scarcely appears at all, though it is accentuated, on the exterior, by the austere but most harmoniously composed fronts. This emphasis certainly corresponds clearly with the interior of the transept, which is clearly distinguished from the arcaded nave. In addition, from the blind arcading on one wall of the transept, above the ground-floor it is easy to deduce that this nave was originally intended to carry galleries, like its predecessor in Basle; also intended was a mighty rise from the nave to the crossing tower. It is clear from the doubled capitals of the crossing pillars, on the side towards the nave, that the arcades of the nave were supported at a far lower level than is the case today. In contrast to the present state, the outer shell of the crossing tower received direct light from the outside: the walled-up windows behind the forward wall of the triumphal arch, for example, show that in the Romanesque building these portions gave on to the open air. The new Gothic architectural ideas, however, rejected the crossing tower, with its effect of emphasis upon the nave as against the choir; and the second master-builder, who added the Gothic nave to the late Romanesque portions, raised it to such a height that the exterior of the old crossing tower now lies inside the building. Thus there came about here a solution – certainly, to the French way of thinking, non-Gothic – of an interruption in the flow of the vaulting towards the choir. Yet at the same time something was achieved which corresponded perfectly with the German feeling for space, and this was also admirably expressed in the later choir.

The builder of the new Gothic nave was obliged to make compromises and we should not so much blame him for the rather clumsy handling of Gothic details – such as the crude tracery windows in the eastern side-aisles, or the great spaces of wall next to the clerestory windows – but rather give him credit for the new conception of space, which certainly drew upon Burgundian models, yet led to a fresh and individual spatial expression. In the nave, in place of what must have been originally square bays, he used transverse quadrilaterals, yet he remained closer to the square than did French Gothic and thereby preserved also the spatial individuality of the single bays, which quality also finds expression through other elements: for example, the smooth closed wall in place of the triforium, and the perpendicular clustered columns which rise from the pillar bases to the shoulders of the vaulting. Through the considerable broadening of the side-aisles to almost double the originally planned width, at ground level the edifice gives almost the impression of a hall-church. The side-aisle walls gain in weight and significance from their rich ornamentation, with trefoil arcades carried upon pillars and themselves supporting an ambulatory before the area of the windows (corresponding to an as yet unbuilt corridor in front of the clerestory windows). The narrow arcade-walk of the nave in French cathedrals loses its extreme emphasis and the side-aisles merge with the nave in an intimate unity.

The arcade piers – here rightly called piers with clustered shafts, in contrast to the simple composite piers – which are particularly characteristic of Gothic in the upper Rhine region, also play a considerable part here. They are found also, in a preliminary state, in Strasburg, though not executed with the same consistency as in Freiburg. These piers are erected upon a ground-plan which is square, but diagonal to the axis of the building. By their consequent projection into the room, they stress the solidity of the wall, since they – more than any previous form of pillar – have become spatial elements themselves.

The plastic mass having thus found its incorporation here, it is almost inevitable that the solidity of the pillars should be augmented by the sculpture set against them. The piers are obviously identified with the apostles as the 'pillars of the church'.

The work of this first Gothic master-builder was soon carried on by a skilled and progressive successor. Where the first had left the two eastern bays of the nave unvaulted, yet had prepared for the vaulting in the traditional manner, with supporting arches under the roofs of the side-aisles, the second now carried out the vaulting of these bays with the aid of supporting arches on the exterior, in accordance with the latest technical achievements of French Gothic. At the same time, the construction of the nave was carried on from east to west and in the west a start was made with the building of the tower, the pinnacle of the achievement of the builders of Freiburg. Its two lower storeys are from the hand of a certain Master Gerhart, who completed the tower up to the belfry level in 1301. Master Henry – Heinrich der Leiterer – carried on the work of his predecessors from 1310 to 1350 and finally produced what was to be one of the most beautiful towers of western Christendom.

The lower storey of the tower, of massive masonry construction, rises to above the roof of the nave. It is almost square in ground-plan and is set before the nave as an independent constructional element; in relation to the side-aisles, it remains absorbed yet the view of the side-aisles is almost blocked by the massive buttresses. These mighty buttresses project in pairs, to the front and to the sides, while in the east the tower is supported with the nave, and behind

125

the jambs of the doors specially strengthened walls are formed for its support. The buttresses narrow upwards in steps corresponding to the storeys marked by horizontal stone gutters. At three different heights, they carry figures surmounted by canopies, which exert an attenuating effect upon the mass of the walls: first attached to the pillars near the entrance, then masking the first step, and finally set before the last, when looked at from below, they produce the illusion that the buttresses terminate in a small, narrow tower.

The tower, standing as it does before the church as an independent element in the structure, and still more the rooms attached to it in the lower storey, make it clear that here recourse has been had to the old German architectural concept of the westwork which possesses – apart from its function as the church entrance – its own autonomous spatial significance. Thus, there opens up, on the ground-floor, a great entrance hall whose entrance is formed of a deeply graduated pilaster-wall, devoid of ornamentation yet filling the entire width of the space between the buttresses and crowned with a relief presenting the coronation of the Virgin. The interior of the hall is surrounded by stone benches, above which rises a finely articulated arcading, set before the wall; and over the arcade piers, between their peaks, are set figures surmounted by canopies, symbolising the decrees of Christianity. These surround the interior space and look down upon the happenings within, yet at the same time point the way to the entrance, for they are continued in the figures bordering the main portal, with its Marian orientation. The entire portal is dedicated to the theme of the tree of Jesse, surmounted by a representation of the throne of God, in which the dream of the sleeping Jesse is fulfilled. Thus there is here created, as in the old westwork, an assembly room in which temporal and juridical matters could be dealt with which should be seen to fall immediately within the field of Christian belief. As in the Carolingian westwork, above this assembly room a chapel is attached, dedicated to St. Michael; and this opens on to the nave by way of a great ogival arcade, above the entrance to the porch, yet in full view of its great and simple tracery window

– which was probably largely masked by the summit of the gable crowning the entrance.

The change from the base to the superstructure of the tower takes place above the chapel of St. Michael, in the clock storey – a change for which the builder of the lower storey had certainly prepared, since he had brought the buttresses with their canopied figures to an end here and drawn in the walls around the central portion. His successor used a star-shaped balustrade, with twelve points, as the termination of the lower portion – the balustrade being supported by consoles, some of which carry portrait heads, presumably those of the men who carried out the work, so that they stand out above the lower tower. In continuation, he erected a high, two-storeyed octagon, the first storey built round the open bell-storey of the earlier master, while the second consisted of a hall open on all sides. The subsequent building up of the bell-storey into a bell-ringing lobby detracts considerably from the original effect, which depended upon the plainness of the octagonal framework. In order to pass smoothly from the square of the lower portion to the new octagon and at the same time to give to this remarkably tall octagonal structure the solidity which it required (including the gables and pinnacles which crown it, it is taller than the tower itself) the architect used a remarkably ingenious method which was just as effective from the visual as from the constructive point of view: against each of the four spandrels that make the base of the octagon a complete square he placed a small slender, triangular decorative tower, firmly connected to the octagon at its base; these gradually narrow upwards, disengage and finally leave the upper part of the octagon free from their embrace. Above the bell-storey there is a high tower-hall from which – since it has no ceiling – one can see directly into the crest of the tower, which, itself eight-sided, rises up behind the gables of the octagon.

The tower of the Freiburg minster owes its special fame as an example of pure architecture, entirely free from the traditional purpose of protecting the interior from the world outside, from rain and from sun, to the grandiose achievement of the man who built that spire. The spire is entirely composed of pierced tracery work, and supported by eight ribs, studded with crockets, which rise up in a gradual curve. The penetration of air and space into the interstitial vacuities of the grille-like structure próduces a corresponding beauty and charm in the view from the interior, so that this tower becomes the fulfilment of Gothic translucency in architecture: substance itself seems immaterial.

Looking up at the western aspect of the tower from below, one experiences the enormous dynamic of the structure, the three stages rising powerfully one above the other up to the inward-curving cone of the spire. The effect of perspective completely conceals the fact that the three main stages – substructure, octagon and superstructure – are of almost exactly the same height; for their relationship to the vertical plane is defined very differently. In the substructure, as far as the gallery, horizontal divisions break up the vertical trend of the buttresses; in the octagon, vertical divisions are clearly dominant and only the abrupt marking of the storey divisions, breaking the vertical line, echoes the horizontal motif of the substructure; while in the superstructure, neither the vertical nor the horizontal is predominant and the curve is the sole visual effect – the oblique curves of the ribs and the diagonal rings covered with tracery in circular formations.

When the tower was completed, the entire structure, with its huge western façade, high nave, and tiny Romanesque choir, must have appeared somewhat strange. The citizens of the town, therefore, decided to rebuild the choir and commissioned Johannes von Gmünd, a member of the famous Parler family, to draw up the plans. The foundation stone was laid in 1354. Johannes was actually engaged in the work in Freiburg from 1359, but he must have supervised the early stages from Basle, where he was restoring the Minster, which had suffered grave damage in the earthquake of 1356. Beginning by raising the roof between the late Romanesque weathercock towers, he made the new choir descend in an almost emphatic step towards the now lower nave. The inner choir he laid out in a long basilical form with an ambulatory and chapels. The building of the new choir, however, made only slow progress, the work languishing for

decades, until in the last stages of Gothic architecture, it was finally completed and consecrated in 1513. Late Gothic vaulting, with ribs in network form, covers the almost hall-like, extended high choir. The burden of the ceiling is borne by a complicated system of supports between the windows, while the visible network rather veils than reveals the static relations. The now in part purely decorative motifs of the ambulatory and the chapels produce an effect of equal delicacy.

The Church of the Holy Cross in Schwäbisch-Gmünd

The purest expression upon German soil of architectural aims in contrast to those of French cathedral-Gothic is to be found in the building of the hall-churches which appear in increasing numbers from the time of the first invasion of the Gothic, and especially from the middle of the fourteenth century onwards. One could compare it with the 'anticathedral' movement in France itself, yet its formal architectural treatments are very different. The hall structure appears simultaneously in many places in Germany during the thirteenth century: in Marburg, from 1235 to 1283, with a host of successors in Hesse; in Paderborn, around 1230 to 1280, in a fashion epoch-making for the development of Westphalian hall-churches; in Minden, in 1267; and in Erfurt, around 1270, with a hall of five aisles. But the hall-church was to find its richest unfolding and its definitive form in the period of late Gothic: in Vienna, with the cathedral of St. Stephen, from 1339; in the Wiesenkirche at Soest, after 1343, in a hall as high as it is broad, yet with small extension in depth; in the hall-choirs of the Parler family in Zwettl (begun in 1343) and in Gmünd (from 1330); in the churches of Dinkelsbühl and Nördlingen, Amberg, Annaberg and Nürnberg and in the buildings of Hans Stethaimer in Landshut and Salzburg – to cite only the best-known examples, whose basic features we shall deal with in discussing the Church of the Holy Cross, in Gmünd. With the beginning of work on the choir in 1351, a turning point can be established in the development of the Gothic on German soil: the standards derived from French Gothic lose their validity once and for all.

The exterior in its ground-plan resembles the form of an extended bath, like that of the Jacobin church in Toulouse. In its geometrically simplified mass, it appears almost hard and unyielding. The western entrance side is composed of a simple, only slightly articulated, gable façade, which corresponds exactly with the cross-section of the interior lying behind it. The characteristics which we have established for cathedral Gothic now appear as faint influences: the

Schwäbisch-Gmünd, church of the Holy Cross: façade

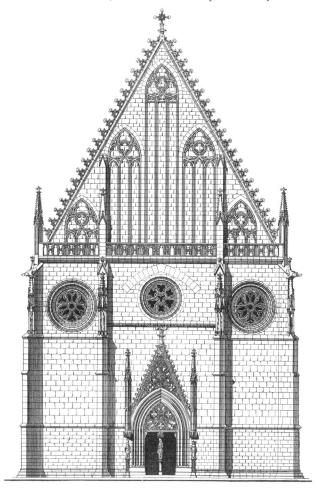

vertical division of the façade into three slightly projecting buttresses, the slightly recessed portal and three rose windows – compared to the rose windows of the cathedrals they have the effect of models – correspond more to the Romanesque emphasis upon the mass of the walls than to the Gothic tendency to translucency. Nevertheless, one is reminded of the soaring character of the cathedrals through the heavy substructure, with its threefold horizontal division and its termination in a stone balustrade which adorns the entire building, and the comparatively light gabled roof which rises up behind it.

The motif of the buttresses, set close against the wall and ending above in pinnacles which overtop the cornice, surrounds the entire structure. Since the interior is arranged as a hall, with nave and aisles of equal height, there are no such complicated static problems as with a nave that rises above its side-aisles. The vaults of nave and aisles of the same height support one another in mutual balance and demand only relatively slight support from the sides. The architect was able to make these laterally set pillars even smaller since he had not completely broken up the parts of the walls lying between them with windows, but by making these relatively small had given the character and function of the walls full validity.

In the exterior, however, it is the choir in which the builder achieves his finest solution and from which the church derives its fame and its position as the prototype for the buildings of the entire Parler family. Between the buttresses, which are here slightly more pronounced, chapels are built up to half the height of the walls. The exterior of the apse, therefore, presents a closed and continuous wall, behind which the choir proper, with its ambulatory, rises up. As a third step there rises yet again, behind the balustrade and pinnacles, the polygonal eastern aspect of the roof which covers the nave and side-aisles as though to protect them. It is on the exterior of the choir that the builder, Heinrich Parler, has lavished the richest architectural decoration that the church has to show; there are broad tracery windows in the chapels, crowned with a repetition of the roof balustrade, gables, twin pinnacles and a double row of gargoyles. Also here in the exterior is a motif which one can find, as a kind of secret family signature, on almost all the buildings of the Parler family – the Gothic round arch. Here, Heinrich Parler has introduced it as a relieving arch, richly decorated with foliage, under the shoulder of the roof and above the windows of the ambulatory, and has thus reminded us yet again and obviously of the eastern side's characteristic rounded wall.

The interior at Gmünd also fulfils characteristically all the principles of the hall-church. The fact that the nave and the two side-aisles are of equal height brings about considerable differences in the structure as compared with a basilica: the central nave loses its dominant character and the formerly so strictly observed orientation of the structure gives place to a more comprehensive spatial unity that allows of a diagonal outlook towards the choir – or, indeed, of a transverse view. Even the pillars of a hall-church have a different function: instead of dividing the nave from the side-aisles, as in the basilica, they unite it with them.

Further, the side walls are of decisive importance for the effect of a hall-church. In a basilica, they take second place to the wall of the nave and are responsible for the latter's spatial background; but in the hall-church, they are themselves stressed spatial boundaries and also have a decisive influence on the character of the space enclosed, by the light which falls from their windows. For light itself plays an important part in determining the character of the hall-church: it is not concentrated upon certain parts, in order to emphasise them, but fills the entire space evenly; the pillars are bathed in light and the formation of deep shadows is prevented. It is not entirely mistaken, in architecture, as in the sculpture of the period around 1375–1425, to speak of a 'soft' style.

Finally, the vaulting, too, is of great importance for the hall-church; like the pillars, the vaults no longer have the function of separating spaces. The hall-church expressly avoids the strict division into bays and, therefore, has recourse more and more to the ceiling structure with a network of ribs that now no longer reveal their static function but hide it. The load-bearing function of the ribs – one of the chief principles of high Gothic – is here abandoned; and

thereby the vaulting of the church is transformed into a pure and unified covering of space.

The return to the high Gothic which took place around the middle of the fourteenth century and led on the one hand to the building of the great cathedral on the Hradschin, in Prague, and on the other to a tendency to portraiture in sculpture – as with the Naumburger master and in the busts by Peter Parler in the triforium in Prague – is also reflected in the Church of the Holy Cross, in Gmünd, in the unmistakeable distinction of the choir, as compared with the nave, which we have already remarked in the exterior. In the interior, the floor rises towards the choir and the load-bearing pillars are also higher – which fact nevertheless is not apparent from outside in the level of the roof. The choir vaulting has a ribbed network of particularly rich design; and the setting-back of the choir with its ambulatory pilaster-chapels leads here, in the lower area, to that translucency of space exemplified best in French cathedrals. This translucency is observable first only at the ground-floor of the choir, but is already suspended in the area of the high windows and takes on a new form in the zone of the vaulting.

The Abbey of the Cistercians in Chorin

A new task confronts the master-builders where the local building material is different from that used for French Gothic, as in north and east Germany, where the tradition of brick building became very early established. Once it has emerged from the kiln, the brick allows of no subsequent working by the masons: when variations from the normal brick form are required, they must be made before the baking. Consequently, all brick-built architecture has in it something of the 'unit' principle.

If the brick buildings of southern France, such as Albi and Toulouse, with their 'anticathedral' architectural mood, are often interpreted from the point of view of the material, one glance at the German Gothic brick buildings teaches us that a close accord with architectural concepts of the Ile-de-France – always taking into consideration the technical possibilities of the material – is certainly possible. A

Chorin, the Cistercian church: façade

the most practical spatial form possible, yet with a high standard of workmanship. Thus the interior of Chorin – although much reduced, in its present state of preservation, by the collapse of the vaulting since the secularisation of the monasteries – is one of extreme simplicity, yet of a masterly workmanship.

The church was erected around 1274 as a cruciform basilica, without a triforium but with the transept prescribed by ritual requirements. It was consecrated in 1334. Certain features of the interior are rather archaic, as for instance the alternation of the clustered supporting piers, reminiscent of the Romanesque system of alternating supports. However, the vaulting takes on a transverse rectangular form and possesses a rib-structure of unique delicacy – particularly apparent at the point of discontinuance of the arching. Since the rules of the Cistercians also forbade an extravagant system of buttresses, these are hidden under the lean-to roofs of the side-aisles.

It is obvious that no contravention of the rules was found in the rich elaboration of the façade; and this component is thus an excellent example of the imaginative form-concepts which can be achieved by men driven by the desire to create, even when they are forced to confine themselves strictly to pure architecture. We are presented with the heavenly city of Jerusalem – in its impression, utterly immaterial and unreal in a way only attainable by a decor of outline and silhouette. Despite the projecting buttresses and the niche-like indentations, this façade remains above all a plane surface, without any perceptible relation to a space or a building lying behind it; it exists independently of the basilica which it conceals, whose side-aisles are far lower than one might suppose from the tall side gables which rise up largely free and unattached into the air. It is the tall, central lancet windows and their flanking lancet-shaped niches and the exclusively vertical divisions rising up to the crown of the gables – all above a relatively heavy and unbroken base – which lend the building its weightless and soaring character. The whole is based upon a hierarchical, tripartite division, the high central nave dominating the two symmetrical lateral components. This generalised principle repeats itself in the grouping of the windows in the

well-known example of the way in which German brick-built Gothic managed to come to terms with France is provided by the Marienkirche – the Church of Our Lady – in Lübeck, which also served as an example for the entire eastern region. In its ground-plan and elevation the church follows the Gothic basilical scheme, with transverse rectangular cross-vaulting, choir with ambulatory and radiating chapels, and open buttressing. In the division of the walls, it was obviously not possible to build a triforium; yet the triforium was not omitted, for in many churches it was painted upon the plastered walls.

One of the best examples of bold exploitation of the possibilities offered by preformed bricks is the façade of the abbey-church of the Cistercians in Chorin, in the Marsh of Brandenburg. The prescribed rules of the Cistercians forbid the erection of towers and call for central portion and again in the arrangement of the two side gables; so that the system of parallel repetition of similar forms leads to a total impression of rigidity. An additional element lies in the astonishing beauty of the architectural details, confined, as they are, to the possibilities achievable by the simple combinations of plain bricks. Nevertheless, we find tracery work, round arches and indented friezes which do not seem to have been conditioned by the material but to have grown out of it naturally by a sort of crystallisation.

Chorin, the Cistercian church: detail of gable

The Cistercian Monastery of Maulbronn

The art of monastic architecture plays a special role throughout the Middle Ages: it is not only responsible for the construction of churches, it is also the expression of life together in a self-contained and self-sufficient community. Since Merovingian and Carolingian times, the monasteries had been the mediaeval bearers of culture, which involved the development of material as well as of spiritual living space. Just as the monastic rule orders the spiritual life into a strict, and systematic programme, the practical limits of the monastic life were very early and clearly demarcated.

The Cistercian monastery in Maulbronn, in Baden, is preserved as an excellent example of the layout of a monastery, with its multiplicity of buildings. The monastery, founded not long before, was transferred here in 1147, during the Romanesque period, and the church was modelled on the Cistercian architecture of France, the land of the order's origin. The Romanesque church, originally built with a flat roof, is an example of the original type. From 1210, early Gothic forms began to appear in the heavy structure of the porch, the southern part of the cloister, the double-naved lay refectory, and the similarly constructed refectory of the brothers. In the period up to the second half of the fourteenth century, the later Gothic takes over with the remaining part of the cloister and the chapter house. Finally, in the fifteenth century, first the church, in 1424, and then the 'parlour', in 1493, were covered over with vaulting with a network pattern of ribs. Most of the surviving farm buildings also originated in the later mediaeval period.

Nearly all the monasteries were arranged on a similar plan. A wall, usually lightly fortified, surrounds the entire area. At Maulbronn, a small Romanesque bastion, with a drawbridge from the early thirteenth century, protects the entrance. This gives entry to the wide monastery courtyard, which is surrounded by the farm buildings, in the manner of an ancient barricade of wagons. For lack of space, all the later buildings are then scattered almost at random, which leads in turn to an inner division of the area. In its loose arrangement of granaries, barns, animal stalls, smithies, cart-sheds, nursery-gardens, mills and servants' quarters, this outer ring of the monastery contrasts strongly with the strict layout of the buildings of the closed order. Continuing the way from the gate bastion across the farm courtyard one reaches the great building of the monastery church – its entrance hidden by a porch – which dominates the area far around. This road to the church, taken now by visitors, was formerly used by the servants and lay brothers of the monastery. The interior of the church was accessible to them as far as the barrier of a rood-screen. Behind the rood-screen was the place reserved for the priestly monks.

The monks, looking outward, saw the spatial organisation of the monastery entirely differently to the layman, looking in – and Maulbronn is a classic example of this arrangement. The centre of this inner layout of the closed order is a spacious cloister, round which are grouped all the building, including the church. On the west, parallel to the entry of the laymen into the church, there is a large cellar and a twin-naved refectory for the lay brothers. Adjoining it, on the north side of the cloister opposite the church, is the similarly twin-naved refectory of the fathers – in marked contrast to the squat appearance of the lay refectory – covered over with sixfold cross-ribbed vaulting, carried by tall strong columns. Opposite this, and projecting into the court, is the octagonal fountain-house, where the monks could wash themselves before and after their meals.

Parallel to the refectorium of the fathers, and accessible from the eastern side of the cloister by way of steps to the upper storey, lies the great dormitory of the monks, whence they can come by the shortest route, by way of the eastern wing of the cloister into the eastern part of the church, to celebrate their offices. Their way leads them past the chapter-house, which is separated from the cloister only by an open arcade, filled with tracery, which allows charming glimpses of the central paved courtyard. Here, on the east side, is to be found also the 'parlour' – the room in which the monks might receive lay visits – and the dwelling of the abbot, with immediate access to the monastery church. The different rooms are thus grouped very logically in accordance with their inner

Maulbronn, the monastery church: profiles of cross-ribs

relationship to the church. Here, too, we find a characteristic of the architecture of the Cistercians – the lack of all ostentatious extravagance, such as towers, sculptures on the portals, and bright glass windows. Its place is taken by the rightly famed scrupulous handiwork of pillars and tracery, fine jointing and a clear, harmonious and proportionate, disposition of space.

Since the order remained spiritually linked with Citeaux – its 'mother house', in France – its architectural concepts are determined by the same source; and these can be traced in all Cistercian buildings over the whole of Europe. The Cistercians also formed teams of builders, which went from task to task and whose traces can be clearly followed not only here in Maulbronn but also in the monastery of Ebrach, near Bamberg – still preserved in its ancient condition and in the so-called bishop's walk (galleried ambulatory) in the choir of Magdeburg cathedral. It was in the spread of Gothic forms, and in the technical treatment of vaulting joints and so on, that the Cistercian architectural concepts – equally with the architecture of the royal cathedrals – permeated the whole of the later Middle Ages.

Latin Gothic

Among the countries whose own strongly developed tradition in building hindered the spread of Gothic, one of the most prominent is Italy. Yet here again it is the Cistercians who bring in the new Gothic forms, in the shape peculiar to them – strict, and entirely developed from the basic architectural form. The first Italian contacts with Gothic architecture allow us to distinguish the following Cistercian abbeys: Fossanova, near Terracina, in the Pontine marshes (1197–1208), Casamari (1217), south of Rome; and San Galgano, near Siena (1218–1310); San Martino, near Viterbo; Santa Maria of Arbona, in the Abruzzi (1208); Chiaravalle, near Milan; and Chiaravalle near Piacenza. The Cistercian influence, however, does not for long confine itself to the abbey churches, but expands thence, spread by Cistercian building teams, also to building projects outside the closed orders. Thus, the monks of San Galgano in the Maremma took part in the building of the cathedral of Siena and gave it its unmistakeable features of Burgundian Gothic.

The Cathedral of Siena

The first stage was begun between 1196 and 1215 and the nave was completed around 1259. An extensive plan of enlargement, which was begun in the fourteenth century, had shortly to be abandoned because of an outbreak of plague which made recruitment of a building force impossible for a long time. This plan produced only a large wall and a huge south façade, in a fragmentary state of preservation. The close confrontation between Romanesque architectural ideas and Gothic forms is clearly to be seen throughout the whole construction; and these Gothic forms, just because they come in the guise of Cistercian concepts, combine very closely with the native Romanesque tradition.

Thus, the Cistercian renunciation of the two-tower façade combines organically with the native tradition which, from its inception, had made of the belltower – the campanile – an independent element, outside the body of the church proper. In Siena, it stands on the south side of the church, from which it is detached while still forming part of the great complex of the cathedral. The Cistercian rejection of open buttressing likewise corresponds to the local tradition of the conservation of the building as a closed mass. Thus, the arches supporting the vaulting in the western part of the nave are hidden under the roofs of the side-aisles; and in the eastern part of the nave, they are applied to its exterior walls in the form of concave wall-arches. The arcades of the nave, with its two side-aisles, consist of round arches of wide span, supported on composite piers. A characteristic feature is that the elevation of the nave has been reduced to two storeys. Directly above the arcades, consoles support a cornice which takes the place of the corridor of the triforium; the half-columns of the composite piers of the nave also end at this cornice, to which they give added support. A pilaster, applied to the high wall of the nave, from here takes over the support of the vaulting. Immediately above the cornice is the high window, surrounded by broad stretches of wall which, on account of the reduction in the buttressing, here carry out a load-bearing function. The alternation of horizontal bands of light and dark grey marble largely determines the spatial impression and lends animation to the large visible wall surfaces. Yet the exaggerated impression of a restless decorative excess, which is given by most photographs, arises only seldom, since the light softens the contrasts. It is almost possible to see here an element, as of French Gothic, which should take the place of the translucency of the walls, since the alternation of light and dark bands certainly lightens and, as it were, dematerialises the impression of closed walls; yet this is no invention of the Gothic, for the chromatic treatment of space through the use of building materials of different colours had been a tradition in Tuscany for hundreds of years.

One of the most characteristic elements in this merging of old and new forms is the transept-crossing, built up into an octagon and crowned with a cupola. The choice of the octagon with false arcades, in the interior of the tower, and open corridors outside, is a decision in the spirit of Gothic, regardless of the fact that the Gothic cathedral rejects such an emphasis upon the crossing. The retention of the cupola itself, however, is a choice in accord with the native Italian tradition, which will remain effective until well into the baroque period. In this spatial centre of the crossing, with its views to the west into the nave, to the east into the choir and into the two compressed arms of the transept, the visitor becomes aware of a further peculiarity of Italian Gothic architecture: the tendency on the one hand to broaden space in a hall-like way and on the other to concentrate it in certain spatial centres, such as the cupola. We shall meet this peculiarity, which contradicts both the French and the German conceptions of space, in many examples of Italian Gothic – even in a late one, Santa Croce, in Florence; it will also become a determining factor of the later Baroque church architecture.

The façade, erected in 1284–99 by Giovanni Pisano, and unfortunately largely renewed – particularly the sculpture – yet gives the strongest impression of Gothic architecture. From the period of Pisano's control of operations, we have the portal zone right up to the cornice above the round window; this section of the building was distinguished, by its almost hard austerity, from the storey rising above it, first begun in 1376, by Giovanni dei Cecco, after the model of a similar treatment in Orvieto. Only the corner pillars, which vaguely recall the French two-tower façade, are carried on above; the pilaster-towers which flank the round window are not a continuation of the pillars of the portal storey, but begin afresh. It is only by reason of this upper portion that the façade produces such an impression of disproportionate size and luxuriance, as against the austerity of the remainder of the building. As in Italian Gothic as a whole – in the façade of Ferrara and the Florentine cathedral, to name but two examples – the three-cornered gable of the antique temple front plays an important part; the Cathedral of Milan is subordinated, in its general design, to the gable-crowned front elevation of the Greek temple. The master-builder of Siena has built up a structure of three gables – of which the centre is the highest and even the two flanking gables rise high above the lean-to roofs of the side-aisles – in order to produce the effect of a false façade. One is automatically reminded of the brick façade of Chorin, which, though basically different in all its details, has a generally similar configuration. The wall, only slightly differentiated in depth, is emphasised in both cases, but here in Italy with a multiplicity of brightly coloured elements, white marble against dark, shadowed niches, mosaic pictures, all transformed into an immaterial seeming picture-wall.

In the façade, the unequivocal didactic significance presented by the door pillars of French cathedrals is lacking; the figures, removed to a higher area, have less impact. Here in Siena, though partly replaced by copies, they originated in the workshop of Giovanni Pisano, and consist of the heralds of the redemption, prophets and sibyls, and also of ancient philosophers such as Plato. The programme of the façade at Orvieto is more closely confined to the portal zone, where reliefs on the four buttresses show, in strictly typological order, scenes from the Old and New Testaments which find their climax in the contrasting pictures of the creation of Man and his Last Judgment. The theological programme is unfolded further in the interior; but here too, it is so hidden and dispersed over so wide a space as to appear to be designed not so much with a didactic intention as to illustrate the story of the Redemption. Above the arcades of the nave and over the consoles of the cornice, the whole succession of the popes is represented in portrait busts; figures of saints stand above the pillars in the octagon of the crossing; and the entire floor of the church is covered with wonderful inlay pictures in stone, showing scenes from the holy scriptures. However, the theological programme appears at its densest upon the pulpit, the place of the sermon and of the clear presentation of the faith.

The pulpit of Niccolo Pisano rises as a central structure in the midst of the great building. It is of octagonal construction, decorated with images and carried by pillars, and every second pillar rests upon a beast which has overcome another and thus symbolises strength. The central column, supporting the floor of the pulpit, shows at its base the seated figures of the seven liberal arts and philosophy. Above the eight Gothic leaf-bud capitals of the arcade stand sibyls, and in the spandrels between the trefoil arches are prophets and evangelists – heralds of the Redemption. The body of the pulpit itself is covered with seven reliefs, representing scenes from the life of Christ and from the Last Judgment; on the corners between the reliefs there are the figures of the seven virtues and of the Virgin.

Santa Croce, Florence

As the church of a mendicant order, the Franciscans, Santa Croce presents an obvious contrast to the cathedral of Siena; yet this contrast serves as an example to illustrate a kinship of architectural and spatial conceptions. The building was completed in 1295 by Arnolfo di Cambio, who is also known as a sculptor. The exterior is simple and austere, yet outstandingly articulated, above all when, from the Piazzale Michelangelo, one sees it rising up above the neighbouring houses. The façade follows the principle of the gable wall and the gable motif is continued on the sides of the exterior, interpreting the heavenly Jerusalem as a city of gables – that is, a city of temples (one should guard here against the association with the gabled houses of northern cities). In the interior, an enormously broad, high nave, with wide ogival arcades above octagonal piers gives a hall-like effect. Here too, the wall elevation is of two storeys, with a corridor carried by consoles between the arcade storey and the windows of the east part of the nave. The space, however, is not covered by vaulting but by an open roof-truss – the acknowledgement by the monastic order of a simplicity in which the model of the early Christian basilicas is still influential. As with these, one reaches, at the end of the nave, a broad transept, with closely set choir-chapels for the celebrations of mass by the monks. The chapels flank the high but narrow choir, so that, looking through the nave from the west, one sees first the flat wall-surface of the triumphal arch, into which open the choir and the two chapels neighbouring it, as well as the two lancet windows above the chapels and the round window above the choir. Everywhere, then, one's glance falls upon walls, which are only emphasised by their openings. When one looks through the side-aisles, the walls appear still more characteristically as hardly articulated and little pierced space-boundaries, though enlivened by frescoes and memorial tablets.

The importance of the wall is still more accentuated in buildings such as the upper church of St. Francis in Assisi, or the Arena chapel, in Padua, where these space-boundary walls become simultaneously the frame of comprehensive cyclical programmes. Here the emphasis is laid upon a consistent contrast with the translucency of French Gothic – itself a contrast with German Gothic – since the effect striven for here is the 'dematerialisation' of the wall-surface through the chromatic effect of frescoes.

Iberian Gothic

In contrast to the situation of Gothic in Italy, the close relations between Spain and France produced a different result. From the beginning of the eleventh century, the Islamic invaders had been pressed further and further back, and by the end of the Middle Ages, Spain had been reconquered. This reconversion to Christianity was mainly the work of French knights and, following them, the French monastic orders, above all the Cistercians, Carthusians, and Premonstratensians. With the founding of their new monasteries, there spread also in Spain a Gothic architecture which betrays in its details the influence of Burgundy and southern France. Catalonia, already a part of the Carolingian empire, was united to Roussillon and thus remained, in the high mediaeval period, a fief of the kings of France. Architecturally, it is closely connected with the south of France, as is clearly shown by the similarity of the cathedrals of Barcelona and Albi. The north western coast of Spain, too, had formed, since the Romanesque period, a channel for the influence of French art: the pilgrims'

Toledo, cathedral: cross-section

road to Santiago de Compostella, along which the faithful of all France travelled to the grave of St. James the Apostle. As well as the monastic architecture, with its already completed transformation of the cathedral concept, a more direct influence from the Ile-de-France had also penetrated here; as for example in the great cathedrals of Toledo, Burgos, and Leon, whose master-builders had studied in France and in which it was desired to represent the pastoral office after the style of the French cathedrals.

Palma, Majorca, cathedral: transverse section

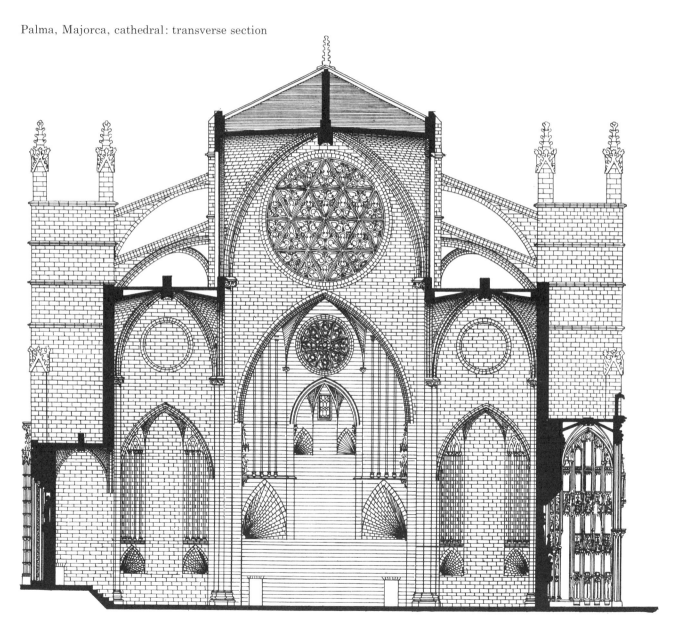

In its basic conception, the cathedral of Palma, in Majorca, is closely akin to the Catalan architecture and shows an unmistakable similarity to the buildings of south-west France, even if somewhat differently executed. The exterior is based on the concept of a defensive building, though without the harshness of Albi. The buttresses are not moved to the interior, but surround the exterior in a close-set row. Lacking the perforations customary in the northern French cathedrals, they rise as closed walls almost to the entire height of the nave, reaching out only from the topmost portion with flying arches to support the vaulting of the high nave. The chapels neighbouring the side-aisles are built in between the buttresses and lighted by a small lancet window. The exterior of these surrounding chapels is hidden by a closely set system of buttresses, which, however, reach only to about two thirds of the height of the piers supporting the nave. Each of these markedly ridged piers ends in a pointed pinnacle, and in double pinnacles in the case of the high pillars. Thus the fortress-like exterior appears as though surrounded by the points of lances – an impression which is strengthened even further by the sharp contrast of lighting produced by the deep, shadowed indentations between the pillars.

The interior surprises by its height and breadth. The impression of close, narrow-set rows that one received from the exterior is here preserved. The high nave, of only two storeys, adjoined by two side-aisles, themselves of considerable height, the slender, octagonal piers which join rather than separate them, and the broad arcade openings give the space a hall-like character which is aided by the plentiful through-lighting from all sides. The impression of height is increased by the fact that the octagonal pillars are carried up, on three of their sides and including the capital section, as far as the spring of the vault. A contrast to this height is provided by the extremely low and narrow choir, which opens into the nave at the same height as its arcades. A great round window with star-shaped tracery above the choir, at the same height as the high windows of the nave, gives one the strange impression that the nave arcades are much higher and the opening to the choir even lower. At

Batalha, the monastery church: wall-elevation in the nave

the same time this window, flanked by similar windows at the eastern ends of the side aisles, does much to increase the lightness and spatial beauty of the interior. The chapels between the buttresses – which we have already encountered in French churches – do not merely form a background for the end walls, but reinforce the impression of a hall-space made up of different heights, since they repeat the relationship of the nave to the side aisles with a similar relationship between the height of the side aisles and that of the chapels, thus producing the effect of a hall rising in different levels. Characteristic for both the interior space and the exterior construction is the peculiar relationship between surface, mass and space. Nowhere can one find anything rounded or modelled, but always an angular opposition of surfaces – on the exterior, sharp, because of the almost exclusive use of right or acute angles, somewhat softened in the interior by the preponderance of obtuse angles. This angular element asserts itself again obviously in the great east window above the choir.

Like Spain, Portugal was strongly influenced by France. Its royal house, in the twelfth and thirteenth centuries, was of Burgundian descent. Just as clear,

Batalha, the monastery church: cross-section

here, as the influence of French Gothic architecture is that of Muslim decorative forms, which remained effective for a long time in all those areas – of Spain also – that had been under Muslim occupation. Here too, abbeys had been founded by Benedictines from Moissac and Cistercians from Clairvaux. After his victory over the Moors, Alphonso I founded the great Cistercian abbey at Alcobaca, with monks sent to him by Bernard of Clairvaux: the ground-plan, the articulation of the walls, the absence of decoration, and the technique of the masonry are closely akin to those of the second church building of the mother monastery in France; and the monastery itself serves as the model for further foundations such as that of Batalha in 1397. It was, however, in the period of late Gothic – there especially rich and inclined to flamboyancy – that Portugal made her own contribution. Its culmination came in the reign of King Emmanuel I (1495–1521), and at a time, therefore, when the Gothic was already being superseded by the Renaissance.

This 'Emmanueline' style, in which Islamic, even Indian, decorative forms mingle with a basically Gothic architecture, found what is surely its most imaginative unfolding in the cloister of the monastery of Batalha. Laid out along the side of the abbey church, in accordance with the usual principle, it is rectangular and includes an inner courtyard, a fountain and adjoining monastic rooms. The openings of the arcades giving upon the inner court are unusually wide, and half filled with a grille of tracery work carried upon five pillars and so delicately worked that one would suppose it to be of wood or wrought iron rather than of marble. The richness of these compositions, the imagination – bordering upon the bizarre – of the play of geometrically decorative pattern, find their parallel (though not their own individual canon of form) only in the English late Gothic. These are marginal phenomena – part of a final phase in the historical development of an epoch – perhaps excessive, but of infinite charm.

Plates

The Hôtel-Dieu of Beaune in Burgundy

143 View of the hospital courtyard.

144 Elevation of the administrative building on the court-yard side.

145 The great ward, in the main building.

146 View of the exposed roof-beams through which the wooden vaulting is supported by the walls.

147 The open passage of the upper storey. The lead flashings of the balustrading can be clearly seen.

Carcassonne (France)

148 View of the castle, a fortress within the town walls. On the left of the picture, the double ring of stepped walls can be clearly seen.

149 Western side of the town fortifications, seen from the castle. The rebuilding work of the 19th century is recognisable where it joins the original structure.

150 View of the double fortification walls: the inner wall is much the higher.

Aigues-Mortes (Southern France)

151 This photograph shows the regular rectangle of the surrounding walls, after the model of a Roman camp.

152 The walls of the town are interrupted at regular intervals by defensive towers.

153 The defensive passage crowning walls.

Krak des Chevaliers (Syria)

154 View from the west of the fortress, upon its hill top.

155 View of the vaulted entrance road to the upper citadel, along the glacis of the south-eastern corner tower.

Castel del Monte in Apulia (Italy)

156 General view, including the entrance.

157 The portal of the interior court, with its severe forms of Cistercian Gothic and its early Gothic crocket-capitals.

158 View of the upper walls of the octagon.

159 Profiled mouldings of the windows and the mighty rib-vaulting are now the most impressive ornamentation in the interior.

The Palace of the Doges in Venice

160–161 The front elevation, on the Grand Canal.

162 Corner treatment of the two lower storeys of the palace.

163 The loggia in the upper storey on the canal side.

164 Courtyard side of the palace. The two arcaded storeys are less pierced and lighted than those of the exterior façade – in particular, the double rhythm of the upper storey is lacking.

165 Clustered columns of the arcades on the courtyard side, with figure-head capitals.

166 View across a spandrel between the arcades of the ground-floor to the columns and tracery of the open loggia.

The Town Hall of Louvain (Belgium)

167 A general view.

168 View of the shoulder of the roof, concealed behind a battlement-like balustrade of tracery.

169 The entrance façade.

170 Wooden vaulting with pendant 'keystones'. The use of wood for the construction of vaulting is common in Dutch and Belgian late Gothic architecture.

Castel del Monte
Plan and section 1:600

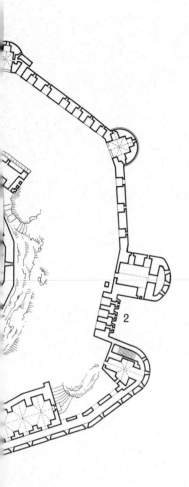

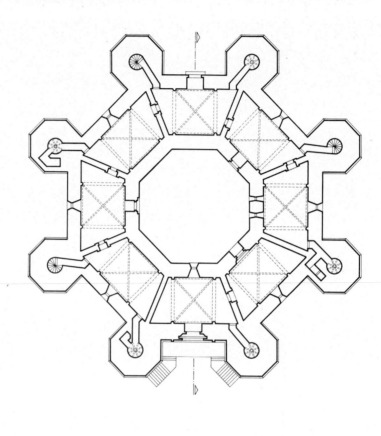

1 Sultan's tower
2 North gate
3 Principal entrance
4 Barbican
5 Main gate
6 Magazine
7 Courtyard
8 Great Hall
9 Chapel
10 Stables and magazines

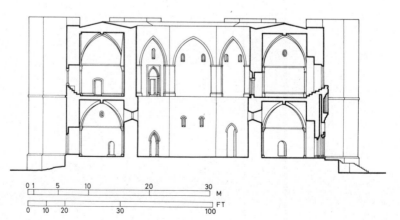

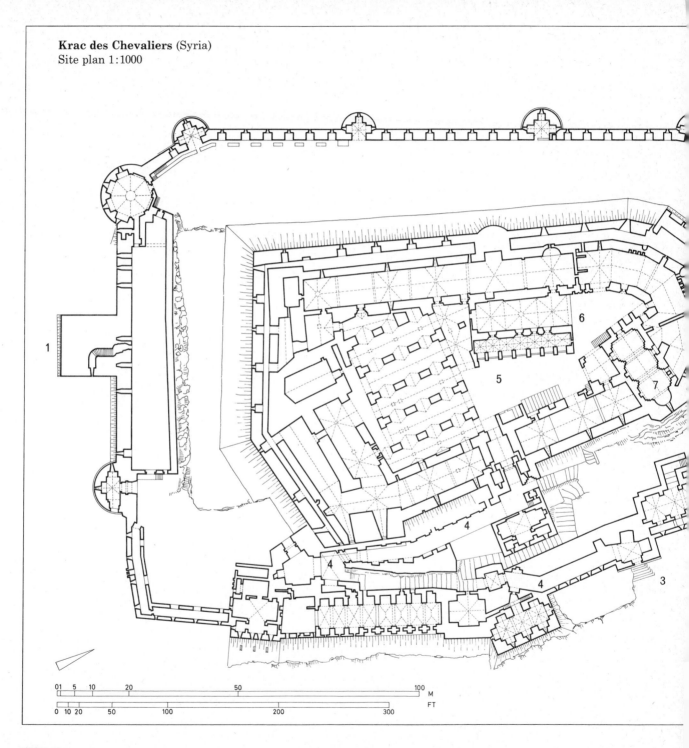

Krac des Chevaliers (Syria)
Site plan 1:1000

1

5

6

7

4

4

4

3

01 5 10 20 50 100 M

0 10 20 50 100 200 300 FT

Notes

Survey of the principal Gothic Churches of Italy

Penetration of Gothic architectural forms into Italy promoted by the Cistercian churches in: **Casamari** (1203–17), **San Galgano,** around 1227, **San Martino,** near Viterbo, after 1215, and **Fossanova,** near Rome.

Assisi, St. Francis. 1228–53. Double church on a cruciform ground-plan. Low-built lower church; above it, a single aisled hall-like space. Passageway above the bonded-in corbels. Wall arcades in the choir; otherwise, emphasis on broad, undivided wall surfaces.

Bologna, St. Francis. Erected after 1226. Choir with ambulatory and chapels. Emphasis on broad wall surfaces in the nave. Clear assimilation of Italian architectural tradition with French Gothic. Under the influence of this church, the **Santo,** in Padua, is created.

Siena, St. Francis. 1250–1326. Single-aisled hall construction; broad transept, with interconnected chapels on the east side. Similar treatment in **St. Domenica,** 1293–1361.

Siena, Cathedral. (See description in text pp. 133–4.)

Pisa, The Baptistery. Centralised construction, begun in 1153; ground-floor with rib-vaulted ambulatory. End of the 13th and beginning of the 14th centuries, completion of the dwarf gallery terminating in a row of gables. Busts by Giovanni Pisani. Completion of the vaulting at the beginning of the 15th century.

Orvieto, Cathedral. Building begun after 1285. Central aisle with open roof-truss. Arcades with round arches, producing an unGothic effect (like Siena) and broad side aisles. Small clerestory windows. Façade designed by Lorenzo Maitani, around 1310. Clear disposal of surfaces chosen as vehicles of pictures.

Florence, Santa Maria Novella. First Gothic building in Florence. Dominican church. Begun in 1283 by the monks, Brother Sisto and Brother Ristoro. Low but broad central aisle, with wide arcade openings. Above the arcades, small round windows. Interconnected chapels on the east wall of the transept. Flat east end. Façade completed in the 15th century by Leone Battista Alberti.

Florence, Santa Croce. Franciscan church, completed in 1295 by Arnolfo di Cambio. High and broad central aisle, with broad columned arcades. In the elevation, a passage carried by consoles separates the two storeys. Above, an open roof-truss. Set on at the east end, a projecting transept, with close-set chapels on the east wall.

Florence, Cathedral. Begun in 1296 by Arnolfo di Cambio. Following his death in 1302, work interrupted; redesigned by Francesco Talenti in 1357, with a spatial division into four clearly conceived bays. Aisle vaults, on a rectangular plan and of half the width correspond with the square central aisle vaults. Building of the east group, with chapels and drum of the dome, after 1380. In 1420, Brunelleschi takes over the building of the dome, which he makes octagonal in the Gothic manner. Completion of the exedra and the lantern, 1436–37. Campanile, by Giotto, begun in 1334. West façade built anew in accordance with the old concept.

Bologna, St. Petronius. Brick built, begun in 1388. Small round windows above the high arcades. Nave of six bays, with double that number of chapels built on to the side aisles. Choir with ambulatory and radiating chapels planned but not carried out. High buttress walls and gable constructions along the sides of the outer structure.

Venice, the Franciscan church of Santa Maria Gloriosa dei Frari. Choir and transept, 1361; nave 1417.
Venice, Dominican church of Sts. Giovanni e Paolo. 1333–90.

Milan, Cathedral. The most comprehensive and the most contradictory achievement of Italian Gothic. Begun in 1387, it follows in its ground-plan the five-aisled cathedral of Cologne. As building material, marble was imported from Candoglio, and was to be worked by Lombard builders, accustomed only to working with brick. Since their experience repeatedly proved insufficient, experts were called in from abroad and were obliged again and again to settle problems of vaulting. The five-aisled, stepped pseudo-hall, with low clerestory, is determined by the dense array of heavy piers and the high area of the capitals, dissolving into figures and baldachins. The exterior is characterised by a decorative vertical thrust and by a filigree of tracery, hood mouldings and pinnacles. Choir, transept and some bays of the nave completed by 1452. The remaining work lasted into the 19th century.

153

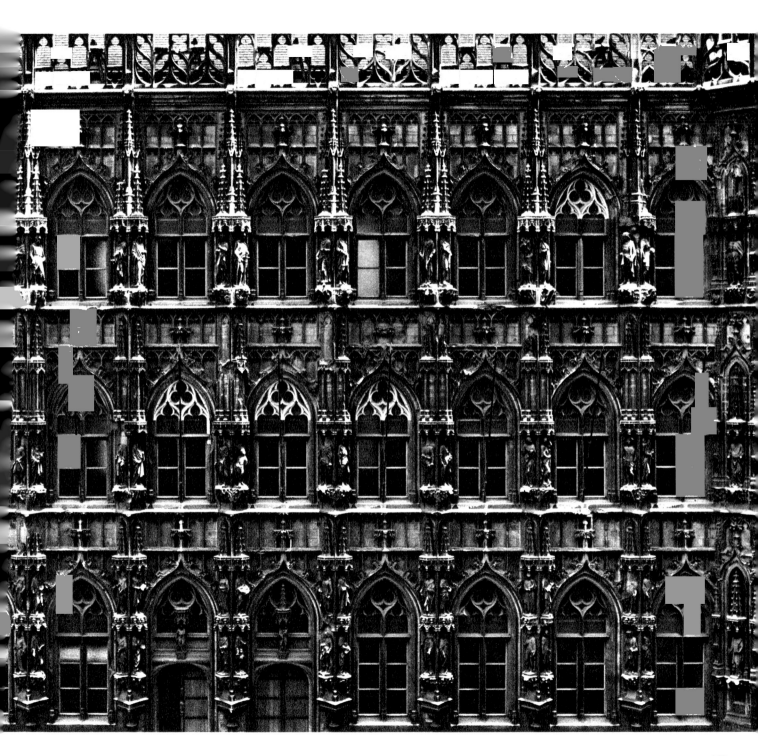

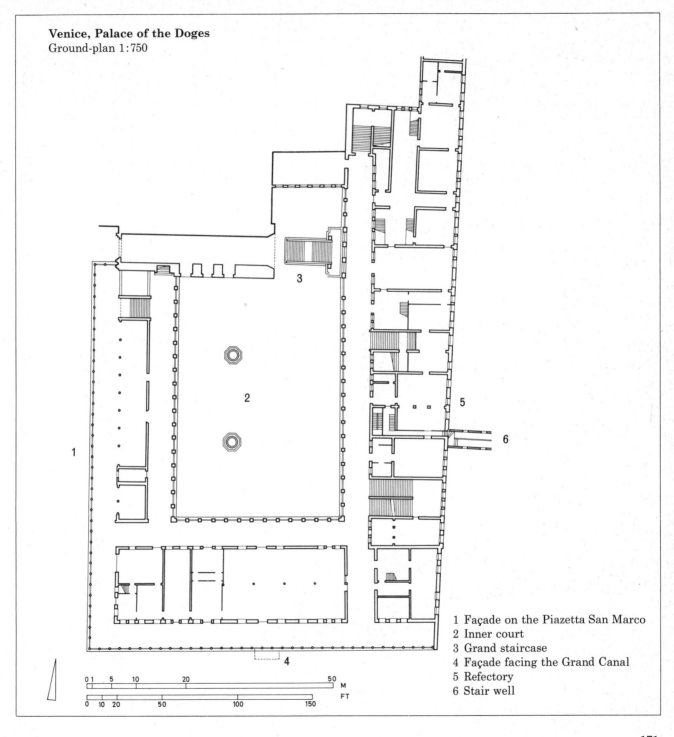

Venice, Palace of the Doges
Ground-plan 1:750

1
2
3
4

0 1 5 10 20 50
M
0 10 20 50 100 150
FT

1 Façade on the Piazetta San Marco
2 Inner court
3 Grand staircase
4 Façade facing the Grand Canal
5 Refectory
6 Stair well

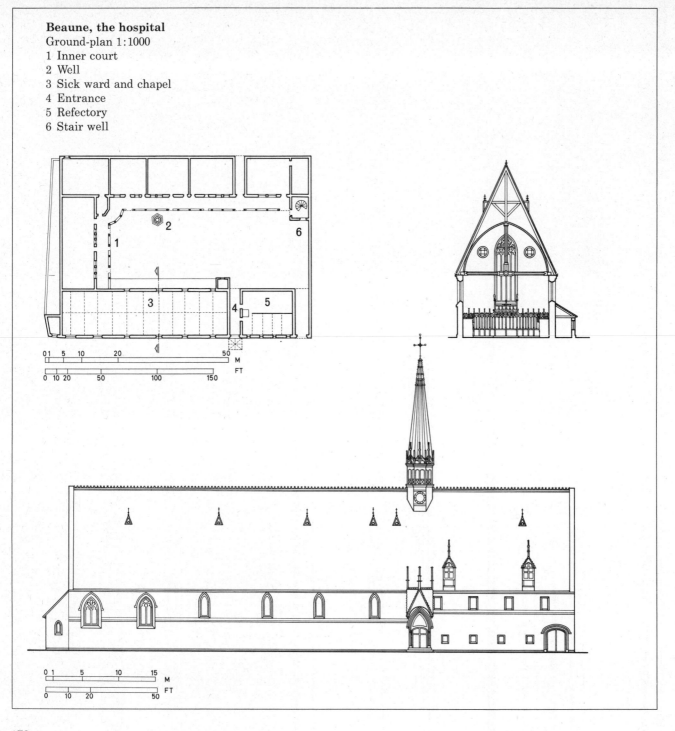

Beaune, the hospital
Ground-plan 1:1000
1 Inner court
2 Well
3 Sick ward and chapel
4 Entrance
5 Refectory
6 Stair well

5. Secular Gothic Buildings

Fortified Towns

The general concept of warfare changed very little during the whole of the Middle Ages, neither did the concept of the mediaeval defensive building. Accordingly, the layout of the fortifications also shows little change and it is easier to distinguish between the various periods of mediaeval architecture by means of the details rather than by the basic structure.

Mediaeval warfare demanded the defence of just those places in which life was normally most peaceful. It was not the victory of the army in the open field that was strategically important, but the securing of prosperous towns or those favourably placed to control trade routes. Strategy, therefore, concentrated on siege, the weakening of the enemy through hunger and final conquest by storm. The defence adapted itself accordingly, using a simple system of protection in fortified cities and in castles alike. There are several rings of surrounding walls, each divided several sections to allow any part lost to be sealed off. High towers watched the enemy's movements; hidden or specially protected sally-ports were constructed for temporary sorties; and great store-rooms were filled with supplies for long sieges. In the layout of the fortified town, as of the castle, there is a specially fortified citadel as a last refuge, to hold women, children and invalids, as soon as enemy attacks threaten to become so powerful that fighting within the fortifications must be reckoned with. In the cities of southern France, this latter function is usually served by the fortified churches, with their right of asylum. In castles, a tower, specially adapted to be sealed off from its surroundings, serves as the last refuge. In the Norman castles of northern France, such a massive refuge tower, called the donjon, is a characteristic component of defensive architecture; in England this tower – the keep – is at the same time the centre of the dwelling of the lord of the castle, while in German castles a narrow tower is preferred, into which to retreat in cases of exceptional need, while normal life within the castle is usually lived in more congenial quarters. Within the fortified towns, the houses are closely set and the streets narrow, since in the case of any increase in population the town must grow inward, the enclosing belt of walls setting a permanent outer boundary to the terrain. The streets leading from the gates to the market place, however, in contrast to the narrow side streets, are kept broad, not only to allow the traffic on market days to circulate more easily, but also, in case of war, to allow reserve troops stationed in the market place itself to be rushed quickly to any point on the walls which may be in danger.

Carcassonne

One of the best preserved of the almost impregnably fortified towns of the Middle Ages is Carcassonne, in the south of France. It was so widely reputed to be unconquerable that even the Black Prince, on his campaigns through southern France, thought it futile to attack its walls. The hill on the river Aude on which the mediaeval town was built had always been an important point for the control of the nearby trade route. Prehistoric finds in the immediate neighbourhood show that the hill was already inhabited in neolithic times and in the Bronze Age. The Romans erected a fort here, but no trace of its walls remains; a mosaic, discovered under the courtyard of the present castle, indicates the existence of a not unimportant Roman villa which, however, lay outside the walls of the camp.

In the year 412, the Romans brought in the Visigoths to settle in Spain, in order to gain their help in holding the Vandals in check; and it was the Visigoths who began the building of the fortified city. Instead of fulfilling their task, they broke through, over the Pyrenees, into southern France, and in 419, conquered western Gaul as far as the Loire. In 462, they also conquered the Narbonne region, to which Carcassonne belongs. Under King Eurich I (466–84), the realm of the Visigoths achieved its greatest extent, reaching for a time as far as Provence. Presumably this king founded in Carcassonne a fortified town whose outer wall must have corresponded fairly closely to the inner defensive ring of today. Many remaining parts of this have been incorporated into the later one; there is even a Visigoth tower still standing on the inner wall to the west of the town.

During the centuries which followed, the town shared in the turbulent political history of southern France. Clovis besieged it unsuccessfully; it was conquered by the Moors and again set free by Pippin the Small. Under the Carolingians, the Moors were pushed back so far towards Spain that Carcassonne no longer played any part as a border town. In the eleventh century, the episcopal see which had been established in the sixth century in neighbouring Bourg, was transferred to the town. At the same time, the first hereditary house of reigning counts made its appearance and built a castle which was replaced in 1130 by the present building. There was hard fighting over the town during the Albegensian wars, in the thirteenth century. In 1226, Carcassonne was surrendered without a fight, to King Louis VIII of France. From then on, the town remained a possession of the crown and became one of its most powerful bastions in the extension of the royal power in the south. Under Saint Louis, the walls were strengthened and the towers heightened; and – most important – the second ring of walls was drawn around the town, with its towers for extra protection, within bowshot of one another – that is to say, forty to fifty yards apart. Under Philip the Bold (1270–85), the walls to the south and the north-west were enlarged, the impregnable Narbonne gate was erected, between mighty towers, and nearby was built the Tréseau Tower, which was to serve the king's seneschal as his command post.

Today, one still enters the town through the Porta Narbonnensis, as through a narrow gully. Over the gate stands a statue of the Virgin in a Gothic canopied niche; she is the protectress of the town. In the choice of the Virgin to protect the gate, we find still existing in the Middle Ages the ancient tradition of the goddess of the city. Within the walls, the houses follow the layout of the ancient streets, but are so much restored that one can no longer describe them as mediaeval. Impressive testimony to the former state of the fortifications comes, however, from the double belt of towered walls, of which the inner rises so far above the outer that an enemy penetration could be driven off almost without trouble from the second position; from the castle, inside the walls, above the western outworks, which is connected to the town by a walled passage and which served it as a last refuge of defence; and lastly, from the Gothic cathedral of St. Nazaire, in the south-west part of the town. Two wells, in the northern and southern halves of the town – the Grand Puits and the Petit Puits – assured the water supply.

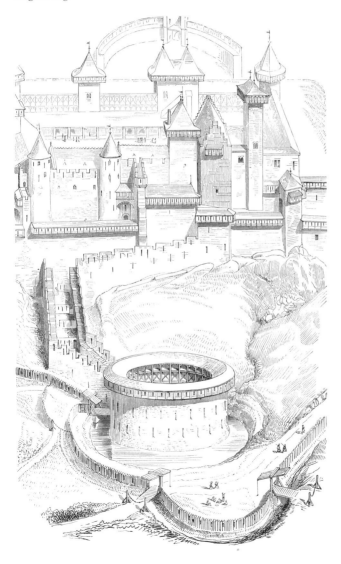

Carcassonne: view of the fortified entrance to the town and to the castle of the counts, after a nineteenth century engraving

It is the restoration work of the nineteenth century which is most obvious today though individual parts of the walls and the towers remain. After the town had finally lost its political significance, in the seventeenth and eighteenth centuries, no repair work was done on the fortifications. The castle served as a state prison, the town itself as an arsenal and barracks. Following the French Revolution, some parts of the walls and the towers were sold for building the houses of the new town at the foot of the hill. In 1850, the destruction of all military installations was decreed, after the upper parts of the walls and the towers had already fallen in. However, public opinion in France rose up in indignation against the measure; and the decree was not merely abrogated but replaced by special steps for the preservation of the town. Viollet-le-Duc, an architect and an experienced restorer, was entrusted with the task of rebuilding the fortifications.

He fulfilled his task with a sober didacticism typical of the historicism of the nineteenth century and corresponding with his positivist attitude to the monuments of the past. Thus, the battlements and the upper parts of the towers, with their conical roofs, which he restored, seem to us all too schematic; for it was the aim of the restoration work to establish a state – historically entirely imaginary – in which all parts of the fortifications were of a uniform style. Such a homogeneity had, of course, never existed; for at all times modernisation and repairs had resulted in the juxtaposition of old and new forms and had thus preserved a total impression of living picturesqueness. Thus, Viollet-le-Duc removed the comparatively recent bastions upon which the cannon of the defenders had been placed in an attempt to reconstitute a fortification of the high medieval period, whose defenders had no knowledge of artillery. In this way he deprived the town of the dynamic impulse of historical change and development and created a sort of puristic concoction such as had never existed in reality.

Aigues-Mortes, the Port of Saint Louis

It is to Viollet-le-Duc, who was one of the most pro-

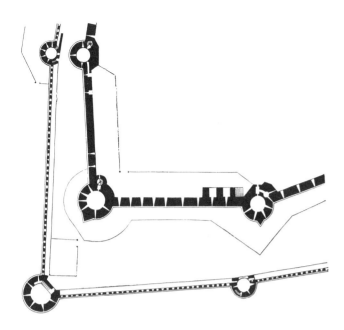

Partial view of the town fortifications, Aigues-Mortes

the town had lost all its importance – a circumstance to which we owe its excellent state of preservation.

An aerial photograph gives the best impression of the layout of the town. No particular conformation of the landscape – as in Carcassonne – needed to be taken into consideration; so an almost rectangular defensive wall was constructed, after the manner of an ancient Roman fort. Its greatest length is 567 metres, the greatest breadth, 301 metres. Fifteen differently shaped defensive towers, each containing two rooms one above the other, interrupt the wall, around which there originally lay a broad moat for additional protection. At one of the corners, near the port, there is a great keep that surely served the king himself as fortress and dwelling during his visits. One should not imagine the space inside the town walls as originally covered with houses, but rather as a vast tented camp for the Crusaders' army, just as in Italy, also, the fortress-refuge consisted of a great open space, surrounded by a huge defensive wall. The church was probably then one of the few stone buildings.

The exterior of the walls is smooth and unarticulated, topped with battlements and pierced with very thin slits, the loopholes for the archers on guard, who sat behind them in a round-arched niche that had a bench on either side. In the larger towers, steps within the walls led to the upper chambers and to the defensive posts above. Almost disillusioning is the contrast between the powerful and harmoniously proportioned fortifications and the present town within, which resembles in character a Parisian suburb. This is quite natural, in view of the fact, mentioned above, that originally a proper town within the walls simply did not exist and the houses of today have been built comparatively lately – mostly in the nineteenth century: it is the paradox of an old town without an old town.

These two fortress localities – Carcassonne and Aigues-Mortes – are typical of two basic conceptions of the fortified town: one follows the contours of the land and is extended in the course of time – in fact, develops historically – while the other is planned on the drawing-board, laid out in a short time and experiences no important later change. There are two

gressive constructional engineers of his time, that we owe the protection and preservation of many of the cathedrals of France; and it may well be that, in striving for uniformity of townscape, he was inspired by such a town as Aigues-Mortes, in the Camargue. In contrast to Carcassonne, however, Aigues-Mortes was – figuratively speaking – built in a day, and its layout has remained unaltered, since the town has never been fought over. Saint Louis acquired the area in 1240, in order to build a harbour for the embarkation of the Crusaders. In those days, the place lay nearer to the sea than today, and was connected to it by a canal. In 1248 and 1270, the king set off from here upon Crusades – the last time with an army of about 100,000 men. Neither of these expeditions was crowned with success; and on the second, the king himself found his death through a plague infection, in North Africa. Philip the Bold, the son of Saint Louis, drew walls, protected by towers, around the area of the town, so that the whole was completed, in all essentials, by the year 1300. However, it became ever more hopeless to prevent the silting up of the harbour; and already in the fourteenth century, corresponding basic concepts in the building of castles: that which is adapted to the terrain and altered in the course of time and the unchanging fort, which is not dependent in any way upon the site. Here we shall describe a typical embodiment of each: Karlstein Castle, near Prague, in Bohemia, and Castel del Monte, in southern Italy.

Karlstein Castle, near Prague

Karlstein Castle, about thirty miles from Prague, which was erected by Charles IV as a refuge and as a place of safety for the crown jewels and imperial relics, was built in 1348–65. In character, it belongs to the order of great fortifications constructed upon hills, of which, among many other examples in Germanic lands, we may cite Eltz, Marburg, Salzburg, Frauenstein, Hochosterwitz, Seebenstein, Rappolstein, and Marienburg. In the combination of its present state of preservation and former importance, Karlstein is one of the most impressive monuments to

Avignon: the city wall, with towers

European fortress building. Its site is alone sufficiently astounding: one travels from Prague southwestwards over a wide and open plain, so that one can scarcely imagine where such a great cone, surrounded by valleys, can possibly arise – until suddenly the land sinks away to a valley bottom which it was impossible to see from a distance and one comes abruptly in view of the towering rock, with the castle on its summit. For someone approaching Prague, who did not know the area, it was practically impossible to find the castle at all. Charles IV who had been brought up at the French royal court and had married a French princess, had already caused the castle of Prague – the Hradschin – to be remodelled on the French royal residence; now Karlstein was to demonstrate the French style even more favourably, in particular the papal palace at Avignon. As with Avignon, the layout is divided into an outer or advanced fortification and the citadel itself, and has as its centre a mighty towering keep, accessible only by way of a narrow entry and thus easy to defend. Security is further served on the sloping side by an outwork, set well forward and furnished with walls and towers. In addition, the precipitous cliff makes the remaining sides of the fortress practically unclimbable.

The decoration of the living quarters and halls in the keep has not survived; but by way of compensation the chapel, in an excellent state of preservation, is a real gem. Gothic ribbed vaulting, with gilded keystones decorated with stucco work, descends deeply on all sides. The frontal wall behind the altar is covered with pictures, after the model of an iconostasis; the remaining walls are inset with polished but irregularly cut semi-precious stones, disposed in the form of crosses. Between the encrustations, the wall is gilded. The private chapel of the emperor immediately adjoins this castle chapel; and here he would shut himself in during Lent, receiving nourishment only through a narrow hatch. The walls of this chapel, too, are encrusted with semi-precious stones; on the wall opposite the door, there is a small altar, with a fresco of an old Italian master of the school of Giotto, showing the Virgin with the child Jesus on her lap and the imperial couple in the act of adoration.

The furnishing of these richly coloured rooms is reminiscent of oriental models, probably transmitted through Byzantine masters. In the middle of the fourteenth century, Bohemia was a crossroads of cultural currents from all over Europe. In the architecture, as in the cathedral of St. Vitus, on the Hradschin, French ideas are dominant; while in the interior furnishing oriental examples come largely into play, such as one sees in the early stages of Bohemian panel painting, above all in the terraced landscapes of the Master of Hohenfurt. Karlstein itself became one of the centres in the exchanges between northern and Italian painting after Tomaso da Modena had been called here and the most important Bohemian painter, Master Theoderic – who had painted the crucifixion group crowning the picture wall of the chapel – had produced the half-length portraits of the fathers of the church, in which his style seems closely linked to the northern Italian style of Tomaso.

Castel del Monte in Apulia

While the historical and artistic effect of Karlstein is based upon the impact of cubic architectural elements building up in picturesque irregularity towards the main tower in skilful adaptation to the terrain, whereby all schematicism is avoided – Castel del Monte is built upon a small hill rising only gradually upon all sides, and by reason of the regularity of the design, its effect is exactly the reverse. The Hohenstaufen emperor, Frederick II, had it built around 1240, as a hunting lodge. Several conceptual elements influenced the evolution of the design. The stark, almost repellent, angular exterior and the much more welcoming inner courtyard are reminiscent of similar relationships in the eighth century desert castles of the Ummayyad caliphs of Jordania; since the emperor had called Muslim scientists to his court, a direct connection may surely be assumed. A simple portal, bounded by pilasters and crowned by a triangular pediment forms the sole entrance to the castle. It is a testimony to the conscious attempt at a revival of the artistic traditions of antiquity which the emperor had stimulated. Thus the portal of the Cistercian church in Fossanova shows excessive height in the

form of a pediment in the antique manner, while the capitals are in a metamorphic form in the development from the acanthus to the leaf-bud shape of the early Gothic.

Historicism of this tendency, which shows itself also in the works of contemporary sculptors – like Niccolo Pisano – was later wrongly interpreted as pre-Renaissance, that is, as a preliminary step in the changes in art that came about around 1500. We must not, however, lose sight of the fact that such conscious returns to the antique tradition took place again and again throughout the Middle Ages, both in the arts and in literature and philosophy, since the mediaeval empire regarded itself as the executor of the Roman, and the emperors thought of themselves as a part of the unbroken succession from the Caesars. These returns to past history took place at different periods and often show little resemblance one to the other; yet they are to be directly interpreted as resumptions of the past – within the spirit of their times and with more or less feeling for the original model. Finally, the nave of the cathedral itself was, at this period, conceived as directly related to the arcade-lined street of late antiquity.

With these oriental and antique elements is now combined the Gothic, which, in the final analysis, determines the appearance of the entire edifice. The choice of the octagon as a basic form is a decision in the spirit of the contemporary Gothic. At this period and later, square and circular architectural components are generally transformed into octagonal ones, as we have been able to see in the example of the construction of the Minster of Freiburg. Thus in Castel del Monte also, the body of the building is octagonal, lying around a similarly octagonal courtyard; and at each of the eight corners there is later to be found a widely projecting octagonal tower from whose battlements the whole of the space before the walls could be kept under fire. Altogether, the layout may be seen to be a construction logically developed from the octagonal form. This prismatic form, with its crystalline angularity and the gradations of light arising from the surfaces, corresponds fully to the spirit of cathedral Gothic.

The number of Gothic details in Castel del Monte

is, on the other hand, extremely small. Each exterior wall has a small Gothic window, giving a free view over the surrounding country. In the interior, a finely articulated, arcaded loggia, similar to the triforium of the cathedrals, surrounds the courtyard; and the inner rooms are provided with cross-vaulting – probably introduced by Cistercian builders.

The Gothic Castles of the Crusading Knights

Although the cause of this diffusion is a religious one, the spread of the Gothic castles was wider than that of the religious edifices. The Crusades of the Middle Ages, in which – in spite of the usually tragic outcome of these undertakings – emperors, kings, knights and common people took part again and again, belong to the most extraordinary phenomena of European history. If one disregards the expansion of the Vandals into North Africa, or the raids made by small bodies of Vikings, these were the first large-scale, systematic campaigns of conquest mounted by the Europeans outside their own continent. One can scarcely hope to find the sole ground for these mass expeditions in the pious ambition to free the Holy Sepulchre from the hands of the Muslims. Rather, the Middle Ages seemed to feel the need for a common destiny to a degree which we can scarcely imagine in the West today, unless we should interpret the World Wars as similar symptoms. Just as epidemics suddenly attacked the whole continent, this sort of collective hysteria spread across Europe with extraordinary rapidity. In addition, there was the fact that such enterprises enjoyed the popularity attached to the chivalric ideal, with all its adventurous connotations, which here became popular and accessible to the poor and simple. Siegfried killing the dragon and seizing the treasure hoard of the Nibelungen, Parsifal awaking from his simplicity to become the protector of the Grail–these seem to have been the models which the Crusades brought within reach. At the same time, since the days of Charlemagne and his famous contemporary, Haroun al Rashid, the orient had been a secret dream-goal of western adventurers, who believed they could find there immense treasures

only waiting for the winning to bring them immeasurable wealth.

In spite of the unaccustomed conditions of life, however, the Crusaders succeeded in establishing a foothold in the Orient and in founding states upon the European model. In Jerusalem, there arose a Christian kingdom as a fief, after the French model, which maintained itself from 1099–1187. Under King Fulk (1131–43), the Count of Anjou, it included the major part of Palestine and of Syria. For easier administration, it was divided into four feudal principalities: Antioch, Edessa, Tripoli in the Lebanon and Jerusalem itself. To defend their dominion and protect the trade routes and pilgrims' roads, the Christian knights built a network of Crusader castles, which were often so close as to be within view of one another. As support points along the roads to the Holy Land, castles were built in Greece, in the islands of the Aegean, in Turkey and in Cyprus. In the thirteenth century, however, the position of the Christian knightly orders became ever weaker, while the Muslims, for their part, became more and more united. Between 1261 and 1272, Sultan Baybar captured from the Franks one fortified place after another; and in 1291, as the fortress of Akkon was conquered by the Mamelukes after heavy fighting, the dominion of the crusaders finally collapsed. They retreated to Cyprus, which had been a French possession since the days of Richard the Lionheart, and where their kingdom was able to hold out until its conquest by the Turks in 1473.

Judging this European expansion into the Near East as a whole, its political results were nil; and this is equally true in the religious field, for the holy places captured from the Muslims could not be retained for Christianity. Economically and culturally, however, the Crusades brought about fruitful contacts between the West and the East, for Christians and Muslims by no means always opposed each other as embittered foes but soon recognised that they could profit from each other. Trade relations made Damascene cloths and metal-ware known in Europe; Arabian science began increasingly to influence western thought. As we have shown in previous chapters, not only architecture and interior decoration but also the representative arts drew a valuable stimulus from the East. With the Crusaders as intermediaries, Byzantine and Arabian architectural forms influenced Romanesque and early Gothic architecture; the colourfulness of the Gothic cathedral window is largely due to the colour combinations of the Orient; and the same is true for the textile industry and the art of the goldsmith.

In the architecture of the Crusader castles, correlations are to be found between methods customary in the West and retained in the East and new conceptions of fortification, drawn from local strategic requirements which were then introduced into the West and helped to determine defensive architecture there also. Thus in the ruins of the Crusader castles, which are usually built above the steep slopes of hills or similar cliffs on the rocky coast, one finds the high, square donjon – frequently, however, with this difference from the European layout, that it did not occupy the point regarded as the last to be conquered but stood rather in the forefront of the defences, to help beat off the first attacks.

Characteristic of most of these castles is the ingenious design of the entrances. Already in the West, there are at these points drawbridges, often twofold, over the defensive moats; strong doors, easy to barricade; and portcullis grills, with the real entrance to the fort hemmed in by two widely projecting flanking towers, as we have seen, for example, in Carcassonne. Here in the Orient, however, the obstacles were increased and, above all, the entrance passageway to the main citadel led over a detour – a crooked path with, for example, an angle of 180 degrees, guarded by covered and well protected galleries from which every enemy could be shot down.

Almost all eastern castles use the system of the double belt of walls which we have already encountered in Carcassonne – almost certainly influenced by the Orient. For speed in building, the closed, round tower was often replaced by an open keep covering three quarters of a circle and turning a closed wall towards the enemy while open on the inner side towards the citadel; and this had also a strategic advantage, in that the foe, having once taken the tower, could not shelter from the defenders within

behind its walls. A further important strategic device consisted of barbicans, which surrounded the fort like small independent fortifications and were connected with it through underground passages or by narrow, strongly walled passages that could be completely sealed off if the barbican were lost to the enemy. These barbicans offered the possibility of sudden sallies; but above all, they made it possible to keep hostile siege machines, such as catapults, at a suitable distance. If the enemy wished to place such a machine within effective range, he was usually obliged to deal with the barbicans in advance. This multiplication of bars and obstacles in the layout of the fort was often due to the small number of defenders available; the more impregnable the fortress, became the less the expense of manpower in its defence. The original example for this sort of defensive system must surely have been the stepped walls around the city of Constantinople, erected in A.D. 400.

Krac des Chevaliers

One of the best known and best preserved Crusader castles is Krac des Chevaliers in southern Syria, upon a hill top falling away steeply on all sides, more than 2,000 feet above the sea, among the foothills of the Djebel Ansarieh. Within sight is the neighbouring Chastel Blanc. The fortress was acquired by the French government in 1927, and has been restored as an architectural monument.

The history of this structure reflects the troubled conditions in the Near East in the time of the Crusades. The dominant position of the place presumably led very early to its occupation as a fortified settlement, yet no conclusions can be reached about its presumed importance in early historical times. The first fortification for which there any evidence was carried out by a Kurdish armed band in the first half of the eleventh century. In 1099 the place was first conquered by the Crusaders, on their way to Jerusalem, then given up and later once more attacked. A siege in 1109 was unsuccessful, but a renewed attack by Tancred of Antioch finally took it. Abandoned once more, the castle belonged from 1142 to the Order of St. John. In 1157, the fortifications were damaged by a severe earthquake. It was rebuilt and enlarged. In 1157, 1163, and 1167, the Arabs unsuccessfully besieged it, but in 1169–70 it was again severely damaged by an earthquake. Thereafter there began a second phase of rebuilding and reinforcement, to which King Wenceslaus II of Bohemia gave his support – among other things, endowing the chapel. In 1188, there was another vain siege, by Sultan Saladin, who had to withdraw his troops after a month. In 1201–02, the fort was yet again badly damaged by earthquake and required a third period of rebuilding and extension. From now until around the middle of the century, Krac des Chevaliers achieved its greatest strategic importance as a support point for the attacks of the Knights of St. John upon Arab territory. At the same time, the castle withstood several severe enemy attacks. After the middle of the century, the Franks in the eastern areas drew back before superior enemy power, and Sultan Baybar conquered a number of castles and fortified places in the immediate neighbourhood. In 1270, he attacked Krac itself, at first without success; but in 1271, heavy cannon, catapults and other siege machines were brought up and after more than a month, the garrison surrendered on condition that they should be allowed to withdraw to Tripoli.

The Arabs could now use the castle for their own purposes. They rebuilt the damaged portions and enlarged the castle by building new towers of their own. So important did the place appear to him, that the sultan himself supervised the work. Until well into modern times, Krac was in use as a fort, even if it never possessed again the importance that it had in the days of the Order of St. John. In the nineteenth century, the structure fell into ruin; and stones were carried away for the building of a village within the shelter of the walls. The French restorers devoted their efforts to the preservation of Krac in its original condition and removed the intruding buildings. Avoiding the pedantic historicism of Viollet-le-Duc, they preserved the Arabian portions of the fortifications dating from the thirteenth and fourteenth centuries.

The ground-plan of the construction takes the form of an oblong trapezium, in which the eastern wall

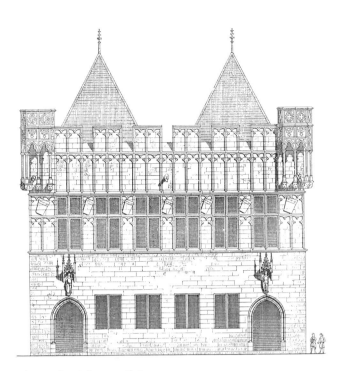

A merchant house, Cologne

runs almost exactly north and south. A second belt of walls, with towers, at a distance of 15 to 20 metres, surrounds the central part of the fortress. In the middle of this there is a great courtyard, which, however, has been gradually made narrower by new buildings – in particular by a large hall with a porch, and by storehouses. The main entrance to the castle, protected in various ways and taking the form of a winding passage leading from the outer to the inner wall, is to be found on the eastern side. It is vaulted over for almost its entire length and protected by flanking galleries in which the defenders could conceal themselves. As the main site of the attack in the Arabian conquest of the fortress, the southern side shows the most marked later repairs and enlargements. Particularly impressive is the form of the bastion at the south-west corner, with the great glacis and the round towers growing up from it. Such sloping glacis surround almost the whole of the inner fortress and contain, immediately behind their walls, defensive passageways and niches with narrow loopholes. Looking through the corridor through which one reaches the castle, one can see here, too, the sloping glacis of the inner walls, with the way running up alongside it.

Münster/Westphalia: town-hall

In contrast to the purely defensive character of the outward-facing portions of the construction, the interior possesses chambers whose Gothic form is derived directly from French religious architecture. Thus, the porch of the hall, with its deep, set groin-vaulting, is reminiscent of a Gothic cloister; and the living-room in the south-western corner tower, called the 'Master's Lodging', has Gothic leaf capitals, a frieze of rosettes, and cross-vaulting divided by graduated responds. The castle chapel, whose apse, at the north-east corner, causes the outer wall of the inner fortress to bulge slightly outwards, shows the most austere forms of Burgundian, Cistercian Gothic. Heavy ogival barrel-vaulting covers the interior space, which is divided by three cross-beams, thrown across it and coming down practically to the floor. A horizontally cut moulding, running around the abutments of the cross-beams, provides an extremely simple horizontal division. After the Arabian conquest of the fortress, this chapel was transformed into a mosque, receiving in the process a prayer niche and another, semi-circular, niche, both on the southern side. Thus, in this construction, all the parts correspond to the purpose for which they were built: the massive strength and severity of the exterior, which reminds one of the cathedral of Albi, to the aim of defence; the light Gothic tracery and finely articulated vaulting to the concerns of everyday life; and the simple form of the chapel to the religious services of the knights under the rule of a monastic order.

Urban Architecture

With the rise of the middle class, came a new desire to decorate the private house also with architectural ornamentation – rich window and door frames, and decorative gables whose stepped form was repeated in the echelonned arrangement of the windows. This desire finds its most perfect expression in the town hall, in which that class finds its supreme representation. Almost more numerous still than those offered by the design of churches were the possibilities of municipal buildings in the countless cities and small towns, whether it was a matter of town halls or – as in the commercial cities – of guildhalls, cloth halls or cornmarkets. The town hall of Louvain, in Belgium, built in 1448–63 by Mathieu de Layens, resembled almost in its exterior a hall for the reception of relics. The pointed towers, their ascent broken by balconies, and the canopied statues which cover the exterior walls, seem rather to resemble chased work than that of the builder. Horizontal alignment plays a conspicuous part in the design and clearly heralds the architecture of the Renaissance, which naturally enough found its earliest expression in the commercial cities.

As a southern counterpart let us set beside it the seat of the government of Venice, the palace of the Doge. Its waterside front was erected in 1340–1419 and the side towards the Piazetta in 1424–42. Here, too, the weighty horizontal articulation and the arcading show those special features of Italian architecture which on the one hand derive from the tradition of ancient Rome and on the other will find yet greater expression later in Renaissance architecture. For this reason, the term 'pre-Renaissance' has been used here, though one should not try to see here any stylistic anticipation but only traditional southern architectural ideas.

The Doge's palace is laid out as a rectangular building around an inner courtyard. From a decorative point of view, only those two sides which give upon the Grand Canal and the Piazetta are stressed; these sides rise three storeys and have a style of their own. On the ground-floor is an open passage way, with ogival arcades upon round pillars, which are separated from the shoulders of the arches above by broad capitals. The result is that the arches acquire in their ascent a lightness which then finds its climax in the middle storey. This is itself of threefold articulation; the zone of the pillars, which is again made to appear superimposed, by reason of the broadly projecting capitals; the arcades, rising in lightly curved, narrow arches, in whose spandrels are set round windows, large compared with the arcades themselves and filled with a quatrefoil tracery. Thus the effect of these two lower storeys is entirely in the spirit of Gothic translucency and lends even this secular building a floating quality, since the massive upper portion rests upon the apparently delicate

Beaune, the hospital: courtyard with well

filigree of the two lower storeys. It is, however, upon this contrast between the two open lower storeys and the closed upper block that the whole effect of the entire structure depends: it has been said of it that it reflects the basic architectural principle of the lagoon city, with its heavy buildings resting upon thin piles in the water. The idea of this comparison, however, is scarcely likely to have played a part in the intentions of the builder, who simply returned to the tradition of northern Italian palace architecture, which he executed with unaccustomed richness and fulness.

Unfortunately, the proportion of the storeys to one

another has been appreciably altered, since the level of the ground has been repeatedly raised, in the course of time, in order to combat the frequent danger of floods, and thus the ground-floor arcades have sunk in relation to it. The closed, upper portion has consequently become too weighty, but the relationship of the two lower storeys has also been altered. A woodcut, supposedly by Jacopo de Barbari and showing a view of Venice around 1500, illustrates with some clearness what the original effect of the front elevation must have been. The contrasting upper part is by no means so massively closed as one might suppose, seeing it in juxtaposition to the open lower storeys, but possesses broad ogival windows, set at wide intervals in the wall, and above them round openings. A central balcony, on which the Doge or state visitors showed themselves to the people, is framed by a baldaquin decorated with figures. A feature of particular charm is the enlivening of the entire wall surface with lozenge-shaped decorations, in stones of two colours, covering the whole area like a carpet. A row of decorative pinnacles forms the uppermost termination of the structure, ascending like flames and once more reminding us of the ogival arcades. It is by such motifs, which are also to be found in the Ca d'Oro, that the Gothic buildings distinguish themselves from the later Renaissance palaces, which generally terminate in a simple cornice against the sky.

The Hotel-Dieu of Beaune

In the Burgundian city of Beaune, there is preserved one of the most remarkable examples – remarkable even for the nature of the building – of Gothic secular structures: the hospital, run by sisters from Mechlin, was occupied by patients up till 1948, while the ancient kitchen is still in use today. The hospital was founded in 1443 by Nicholas Rolin, the chancellor of Burgundy, and his wife, Guigone de Salins, and was intended to care first of all for the sick poor. Unaffected by the low social standing of the patients, the founders caused to be erected a building of almost princely elegance; the elegance is expressed especially in the architecture of the quadrangular

courtyard round which the hospital is laid out. On the street side, the structure is closed off by the great hall-building, with its massive and only slightly articulated walls and its high slate-covered roof. The entrance – through a pointed arch surrounded by mouldings – lies beneath a Gothic canopied roof.

Within this structure is the great ward for the sick, covered over with wooden, pointed barrel-vaulting; and along its walls ran the berth-like tester beds, the curtains of which could be drawn to. In the rear part of the ward, separated from it only by an wooden grill that opens, is the chapel, in which the offices were read for the sick, who could take part without leaving their beds. The picturesque front of the building lying opposite to and parallel with this hall – which held, among other things, the treatment rooms, dispensary and kitchens – determines the effect of the entire courtyard. Here, too, the roofs are set very low, but in contrast to the grey slate roof of the hall, richly enlivened by a design of coloured glazed tiles – a typical Burgundian speciality. Before the walls is set a passageway, open to the courtyard, whose pillars bear an upper passage, decorated with panel work and protected against the rain by the extended eaves of the roof. Since only a few of the rooms had connecting doors, these covered ways allowed the sisters to reach them protected from the weather. The whole front is enlivened by large gabled dormer windows and crowned by pinnacles. All those parts of the wooden construction which are especially exposed to the rain are protected by lead coatings, and leaden crockets decorate the crests of the window gables. The layout around a rectangular court and the allocation of the various rooms may perhaps, in most respects, correspond to the general scheme of mediaeval hospital building, but the execution shows particularly clearly the special character of Burgundian architectural ideas, with their tendency to intimate and picturesque charm, attained not through uniformity but by the decorative distinction and emphasis of individual elements. It is these qualities which explain the wide diffusion of Burgundian architecture, through whose mediation the Gothic penetrated into many of the countries of Europe.

Dates in Architectural History

1137–1140	St. Denis, west front and choir
1134–1155	Chartres, the west portal, including the window group and the north tower
1163–1182	Paris, Notre-Dame, choir
1170–1190	Laon, western bays of the nave and extension of the choir.
1180–1239	Wells, nave
1190	Paris, nave
1192–1233	Lincoln, reconstruction of the cathedral
1195–1220	Chartres, nave and extended choir
1210–1241	Rheims, choir and transept
1209 et seq.	Magdeburg begun. Bishops' walk 1220
1221	Burgos (Spain) begun
1220–1236	Amiens, west façade and nave
1220–1230	Maulbronn, cloister
1227	San Galgano, Cistercian church
1228–1253	Assisi, San Francesco
1240	Castel del Monte
1243–1248	Paris, Sainte-Chapelle
1245–1260	London, Westminster Abbey, choir
1247–1275	Beauvais, choir; collapse of the choir, 1284
1248–1322	Cologne, cathedral
1256–1280	Lincoln, angels' choir
1260 et seq.	Freiburg im Breisgau, tower, 1270–1350
1259	Siena, nave completed
1273–1300	Chorin
1276 et seq.	Strasburg, west façade
1282 to end of 14th cent.	Albi, cathedral
1292 et seq.	Toulouse, Jacobin church
1294	Florence, Santa Croce begun
1296	Florence, cathedral begun
1300 et seq.	Lübeck, Church of the Virgin Mary
1306	Amsterdam, Oude Kerk consecrated
1309–1404	Venice, Palace of the Doges
1310	Freiburg im Breisgau, octagon of the tower
1312	Antwerp, cathedral begun
1328	Barcelona, Santa Maria del Mar
1334–1342	Avignon, Papal Palace
1334	Chorin, Cistercian church consecrated
1334	Florence, Campanile of the cathedral begun
1344	Prague, foundation stone of St. Vitus cathedral laid; Peter Parler in charge of building operations from 1352

1355–1414	Aachen, choir of the Minster
1361–1372	Nürnberg, hall choir in St. Sebald
1368	Milan, castle of the Visconti
1376	Bruges, the town-hall begun
1377 to end of 15th cent.	Ulm, Minster
1383	Oxford, New College Chapel
1386–1813	Milan, cathedral
1397–1498	Landshut, St. Martin, by Hans Stethaimer
1388	Building of St. Petronius begun
1401	Brandenburg, Church of St. Catherine begun
1401–1455	Brussels, the town-hall
1403–1506	Seville, cathedral
1417	Gerona, nave of the cathedral
c. 1421	Venice, Ca d'Oro
1425	Ghent, building of the Cloth Hall begun
1426–1547	Tours, west façade of the cathedral
1427 et seq.	Nördlingen, Georgskirche
1430–1483	Oxford, Divinity School
1441–1447	Cologne, der Gürzenich
1445–1472	Nürnberg, hall choir of St. Lawrence's Church
1446–1515	Cambridge, King's College Chapel
1447–1463	Louvain, the town-hall
1448–1499	Dinkelsbühl, St. George's church
1465–1506	Zwickau, Church of the Virgin Mary
1466–1478	Lübeck, Holstentor
1468–1488	Munich, Frauenkirche
1482–1492	Valladolid, Colegio Mayor de Santa Cruz
1484–1501	Freiberg, cathedral
1499–1525	Annaberg, Annenkirche

Climax of the development of the Hansa, in the Treaty of Stralsund. Revolutionary change to the new age in the reign of Maximilian I, 1493–1519.
Discovery of printing by Johannes Gutenberg, 1440–50.

France
At the beginning of the 15th century, rivalry between the dukes of Burgundy and Orléans for the leadership of the state. Capture of Paris by the English, 1418.
1429, Joan of Arc frees Orléans. Coronation of Charles VII in Rheims. Superiority over the English becomes gradually established. Louis XI, 1461–83. 1477, overthrow of Charles the Bold of Burgundy by the crown.

England
Henry V, 1413–22; Treaty of Troyes, 1420. Henry VI, 1422–61. Around the middle of the fifteenth century: end of the Hundred Years' War with France. 1461, the House of York attains the throne in the person of Edward IV. Following his death, murder of his sons and heirs by Richard III, 1483–85. Battle of Bosworth Field, 1485. Wars of the Roses.

Italy
Supremacy of the Medici in Florence, the Este in Ferrara, the Gonzaga in Mantua and the Visconti in Milan. Alexander VI, the Borgia pope, 1492–1503. Climax of the power of Venice in the 15th century. Decline in the importance of Genoa.

Chronological Table

Historical Events

2th century In Germany, the Hohenstaufen emperors, 1138–1250. (Conrad III, 1138–52; Frederick I, Barbarossa, 1152–90; Henry VI, 1190–97; Frederick II, 1215–50.) 3rd Crusade, with Barbarossa, 1189–93. – In France, the whole of the west falls to England through Eleanor of Aquitaine, wife of Henry II. Philip II, Augustus, 1180–1223. – In England, the Plantagenet kings, 1154–89. Constitutions of Clarendon, 1164. Murder of Thomas à Becket, 1170. Richard the Lionheart, 1189–99. John I, Lackland, 1199–1216. – The Papal state: zenith of the papal power under Innocent III, 1198–1216.

13th century Germany

The 4th Crusade, 1202–04. The conquests of Jenghis Khan, on the eastern borders of the empire. Battle of Liegnitz, 1241. 5th Crusade, 1228–29. 6th Crusade, 1248–54. Conrad IV, 1250–54. Execution of Conradin, 1268. Interregnum 1256–73. Dissolution of Germany into territorial principalities. Rudolph of Hapsburg, 1273–91. Adolph of Nassau, 1292–98. Albert I, 1298–1308.

France

1209–29, the Albigensian Wars. Louis IX ('Saint Louis') 1226–70, conquest of Provence and of the earldom of Toulouse. Philip IV, 'The Fair', 1284–1314. France at the high point of her power in the Middle Ages.

England

Magna Carta, 1215. Henry III, 1216–72. Revolt of the barons, 1258–65. Edward I, 1272–1307.

The Papal State and Italy

Lateran Synod, 1215. Foundation of the mendicant orders: the Dominicans (papal confirmation, 1216), the Franciscans (1223). Charles of Anjou reigns over southern Ita from Naples, 1266–84. The Sicilian Vespe 1282. Italy, gradually falling apart into sm states, is split by the conflict between t Guelphs and the Ghibellines.

14th century Germany

Charles IV, 1347–78, resides in Prague. T Golden Bull, of 1356, elevates the College Electors to the highest governmental bo The intervention of the Pope is reject Dynastic politics of the individual sta flourish. 1315, victory of the Swiss Confed ation at Morgarten. Eastern colonisation the Teutonic Knights.

France

The House of Valois reigns from 1328–14 1338, beginning of the Hundred Years W with England. Philip the Bold of Burgun 1342–1404; defeats by England at Cré 1346, and Poitiers, 1356.

England

Edward II, 1307–27; Edward III, 1327– Hundred Years War with France. Treaty Paris, 1349–50.
The Plague in England, Richard II, 137 99; Henry IV, Lancaster, 1399–1413.

The Papal State and Italy

1303, Pope Boniface VIII taken capti 1309–77, transfer of the papal seat to A gnon. 1347–54, Cola di Rienzo in Rome. Da Alighieri, 1265–1321; Petrarch, 1304– Boccaccio, 1313–75.

15th century Germany

Polish victory over the Teutonic Knights Tannenberg, 1410. Fall of the state of t knightly orders, in the second Treaty Thorn, 1466.

Art-Historical Development

Rapid spread of Gothic from France over the whole of Europe and even into the Orient. The foundation of the Cistercian order in Burgundy and the daughter houses in every country brings about a marked uniformity of monastic building. With the high Gothic, the episcopal churches (cathedrals) take over the artistic leadership. Influenced by cathedral architecture, sculpture develops a monumental character. Gradual retreat of fresco painting through the lightening of walls; stained glass develops in its place.

Age of classical cathedral architecture in France, with the scholastic programme of imagery in sculpture and stained glass. Simultaneously, Germany experiences a late blooming of Romanesque architecture. In the Rhineland, there appears a transitional style attempting to combine Romanesque detail with Gothic lightening of the walls. In sculpture, there takes place an increasing freeing of the figure from strict architectonic bounds into ever more independent forms of human individuality. This reaches its climax in the work of the Naumburger Master. At the same time, miniature carving in ivory begins to flourish in Paris.

Panel painting spreads from Italy outwards, in the form of monumental painted pictures of crucifixions, virgins, and saints. With such painted additions to the altar, we may see the rise of the altarpiece.

The architectural leadership is taken over from the cathedrals (episcopal churches) by the middle-class parish church. Artistic treatment of secular buildings becomes more and more common. The 'decorated style' in English architecture. The hall-church now attains greater significance as against the basilical type.

Sculpture becomes strongly influenced by mystical tendencies. The realism of the thirteenth century is abandoned and images are created intended for meditative devotion and appealing to the sympathies. The body is fully hidden by the garment; figures curve restlessly, as though controlled by external laws.

Around the middle of the century, under the influence of the Parler family of architects and sculptors, the art once more finds stability and the power of realistic expression.

Painting comes to a particularly decisive turning point at the beginning of the century, through Giotto, who produces a new kind of picture, shut off, framed in and experienced spatially. The seeds of his ideas bear fruit throughout the whole of western painting, but presently give way to a mystical, unrealistic mood, until – from the middle of the fourteenth century and above all at the courts of Avignon, Burgundy and Prague – the trend to realism of artistic conception renews itself.

While Italy, with its early Renaissance in the fifteenth century clearly leads on, in matters of style, into the new age, the remaining countries are still tied to the mediaeval Gothic tradition. From the middle of the fifteenth century, we find the 'perpendicular' style in England, corresponding to the French 'style flamboyant' – the 'flame' style, so called from the flame-like form of the tracery. New decorative plastic forms in architecture are combined with already existing basic conceptions. From the point of view of art history, buildings representative of the middle class, together with their dwelling houses, play an ever more important role.

Around 1400, sculpture undergoes a return to the mystical, in the shape of the 'soft' style, with the emphasis upon lyrical elements. About 1420-30, this style is superseded by the 'hard' or angular style – also called the 'Knitter' or 'crease' style, from the treatment of drapery. Towards the end of the century, we find large carved altars and self-portraits of sculptors. From a new feeling for individuality, biblical figures, too, are conceived as personalities.

Efforts towards a new realism are apparent in sculpture and soon also in panel painting, above all since the technical enrichment arising from the use of resinous pigments. Like Giotto in 1300, in 1420 Van Eyck is the key figure of European painting. Perspective, landscape and portraiture are the great developments before the turning point into the New Age.

Bibliography

I. General Works

Aubert, M.
Hochgotik, Kunst der Welt, Die Kulturen des Abendlandes.
Baden-Baden, 1963 (with a comprehensive bibliography)

Frankl, P.
The Gothic, Literary Sources and Interpretations
through eight Centuries. Princeton, 1960

Hashagen
Zur ideengeschichtlichen Stellung des staufischen
Zeitalters, in «Deutsche Vierteljahresschrift für
Literaturwissenschaft und Geistesgeschichte», 9 (1931)
pp. 350 et seq.

Lortz, J.
Geschichte der Kirche, in «Ideengeschichtliche Betrach-
tung», 2 vols., Münster, 1962–64

Mâle, E.
L'art religieux du XIIIᵉ siècle en France. Etude sur
l'iconographie du Moyen Age. Paris, 1910
L'art religieux de la fin du Moyen Age en France.
Paris, 1922

II. Architecture

Bandmann, G.
Mittelalterliche Architektur als Bedeutungsträger.
Berlin, 1951

Behling, L.L.
Gestalt und Geschichte des Masswerkes, in «Die Gestalt»,
issue no. 16, Halle a.S., 1944

Dehio-Bezold, G.
Die kirchliche Baukunst des Abendlandes, vol. II.
Stuttgart, 1901

Frankl, P.
Baukunst des Mittelalters (Handbuch der Kunstwissen-
schaft). Potsdam, 1926

Gross, W.
Die abendländische Architektur um 1300. Stuttgart, 1948

Jantzen, H.
Die Gotik des Abendlandes. Cologne, 1962

Panofsky, E.
Gothic Architecture and Scholasticism. Latrobe, 1951

Rose, H.
Die Baukunst der Zisterzienser. Munich, 1916

Sauer, J.
Die Symbolik des Kirchengebäudes und seiner Ausstat-
tung. 1924

Sedlmayr, H.
Die Entstehung der Kathedrale. Zurich, 1950

France

Branner, R.
Burgundian Gothic Architecture. London, 1960

Guilhermy, B. de
Les Jacobins de Toulouse, in «Annales archéologiques»,
6 (1847)

Hahnloser, H.R.
Villard de Honnecourt. Vienna, 1935

Jantzen, H.
Kunst der Gotik: Klassische Kathedralen Frankreichs:
Chartres, Reims, Amiens. Hamburg, 1957

Kunze, H.
Das Fassadenproblem der französischen Früh- und
Hochgotik (Strasburger Diss.). Leipzig, 1912

Lambert, E.
L'église et le couvent des Jacobins de Toulouse et
l'architecture dominicaine en France, in «Bulletin
monumental», 104, 1945

Laran, J.
La cathédrale d'Albi. Paris. No date

Viollet-le-Duc, E.
Dictionnaire raisonné de l'architecture française du
XIᵉ au XVIᵉ siècle. 10 vols. Paris, 1854 et seq.

England

Barr, E.
Grosse englische Kathedralen. Stuttgart, 1962

Bond, F.
Gothic Architecture in England. London, 1906

Cook, G. H.
English Cathedral Series. London, 1948 et seq.

Escher, K.
Englische Kathedralen. Berlin and Munich. 1929

Harvey, J. H.
Gothic England. London, 1947

Harvey, J. H., and Felton, H.
The English Cathedrals. London, 1950

Hürlimann, M., Meyer, P.
Englische Kathedralen. Zurich, 1948

Moore, C. H.
The Mediaeval Church-Architecture of England.
New York, 1912

Prior, E. S.
History of Gothic Art in England. London, 1900

Saunders, O. E.
A History of English Art in the Middle Ages.
Oxford, 1932

Webb, G. F.
Gothic Architecture in England. London, 1951

Webb, G. F.
Architecture in Britain: The Middle Ages. London, 1956

Germany, Switzerland, Austria

Burmeister, W.
Norddeutsche Backsteindome. Berlin, 1930
Die westfälischen Dome. Munich-Berlin, 1950

Dörrenberg, J.
Das Zisterzienserkloster Maulbronn. Würzburg, 1938

Eydoux, H. B.
L'architecture des églises cisterciennes d'Allemagne.
Paris, 1952

Fechter, P.
Deutsche Backsteingotik. Königsberg, 1934

Gall, E.
Die gotische Baukunst in Frankreich und Deutschland.
1925

Gerstenberg, K.
Deutsche Sondergotik. Munich, 1913

Hahn, H.
Die frühe Kirchenbaukunst der Zisterzienser.
Frankfurt am Main, 1957

Jantzen, H.
Das Münster zu Freiburg i. Br. Burg, 1929

Krautheimer, R.
Die Kirchen der Bettelorden in Deutschland. Cologne,
1925

Spain and Portugal

Balbas, L. T.
Arquitectura Gótica (Ars Hispaniae VII).
Madrid, 1952 (with comprehensive bibliography)

Enlart, C.
Les origines françaises de l'architecture gothique
en Espagne et Portugal, in «Bulletin archéologique»,
1894

Lambert, E.
L'art gothique en Espagne aux XIIe et XIIIe siècles.
Paris, 1931

Lavedan, P.
L'architecture gothique religieuse en Catalogne,
Valence et Baléares. Paris, 1935

Marqués de Lozoya, L. F.
El arte gótico en España. Barcelona, 1935

Secular and fortified buildings

Cahen, Cl.
La Syrie du Nord à l'époque des Croisades et la
Principauté franque d'Antioche (Inst. franç. Damas,
Bibl. Orient I). Paris, 1940

Deschamps, P.
Les Châteaux des Croisés en Terre Sainte, vol. 1:
Le Krac des Chevaliers. Paris, 1934

Ebhardt, P.
Die Wehrbau Europas im Mittelalter. Versuch einer
Gesamtdarstellung der europäischen Burgen. Vol. L.
Berlin, 1939, vol. 2, 1 & 2, Stollham, 1958–59

Ebersolt, J.
Orient et Occident. Recherches sur les influences
byzantines et orientales en France pendant les Croisades.
Paris-Bruxelles, 1929

Enlart, C.
Les Monuments des Croisés dans le Royaume de Jérusa-
lem. Architecture religieuse et civile (Text 2 vols.,
illustr. 2 vols.). Paris, 1926–27

Leflaive, A.
L'Hôtel-Dieu de Beaune et les Hospitalières. Paris, 1959

Printed in Switzerland